Bernd-Ludwig Wenning

Context-Based Routing in Dynamic Networks

VIEWEG+TEUBNER RESEARCH

Advanced Studies Mobile Research Center Bremen

Herausgeber | Editors:
Prof. Dr. Otthein Herzog
Prof. Dr. Carmelita Görg
Prof. Dr.-Ing. Bernd Scholz-Reiter

Das Mobile Research Center Bremen (MRC) erforscht, entwickelt und erprobt in enger Zusammenarbeit mit der Wirtschaft mobile Informatik-, Informations- und Kommunikationstechnologien. Als Forschungs- und Transferinstitut des Landes Bremen vernetzt und koordiniert das MRC hochschulübergreifend eine Vielzahl von Arbeitsgruppen, die sich mit der Entwicklung und Anwendung mobiler Lösungen beschäftigen. Die Reihe „Advanced Studies" präsentiert ausgewählte hervorragende Arbeitsergebnisse aus der Forschungstätigkeit der Mitglieder des MRC.

In close collaboration with the industry, the Mobile Research Center Bremen (MRC) investigates, develops and tests mobile computing, information and communication technologies. This research association from the state of Bremen links together and coordinates a multiplicity of research teams from different universities and institutions, which are concerned with the development and application of mobile solutions. The series "Advanced Studies" presents a selection of outstanding results of MRC's research projects.

Bernd-Ludwig Wenning

Context-Based Routing in Dynamic Networks

VIEWEG+TEUBNER RESEARCH

Bibliographic information published by the Deutsche Nationalbibliothek
The Deutsche Nationalbibliothek lists this publication in the Deutsche Nationalbibliografie;
detailed bibliographic data are available in the Internet at http://dnb.d-nb.de.

Dissertation Universität Bremen, 2009

Gedruckt mit freundlicher Unterstützung des
MRC Mobile Research Center der Universität Bremen

Mobile Research Center

Printed with friendly support of
MRC Mobile Research Center, Universität Bremen

1st Edition 2010

Editorial Office: Ute Wrasmann | Anita Wilke

Vieweg+Teubner Verlag is a brand of Springer Fachmedien.
Springer Fachmedien is part of Springer Science+Business Media.
www.viewegteubner.de

Cover design: KünkelLopka Medienentwicklung, Heidelberg
Printing company: STRAUSS GMBH, Mörlenbach
Printed on acid-free paper
Printed in Germany

ISBN 978-3-8348-1295-7

Preface

Now that the work on this thesis comes to an end, it is time for some personal words.

First of all, I would like to thank Prof. Dr. Carmelita Görg for providing me the position as a research assistant in her working group and thereby giving me the opportunity to do the research work that led to this thesis. As significant parts of this thesis are based on research work that I did for subproject B1 of the Collaborative Research Center (CRC) 637, I also express my thanks to Prof. Dr. Bernd Scholz-Reiter as the speaker of this CRC and as the subproject leader in cooperation with Prof. Dr. Görg.

I would like to thank Dr. Andreas Timm-Giel for many fruitful and guiding discussions and for proof-reading my thesis. He has given me a lot of valuable input and suggestions that helped me to complete this work.

Dr. Dirk Pesch deserves my special thanks for providing me the opportunity to spend three months at the CIT in Cork, Ireland. This time was an interesting and valuable experience for me. I also thank Dr. Pesch for agreeing to be the second examiner for my thesis.

Research is best done in a team of colleagues with whom ideas can be developed and discussed. I hereby express my thanks to all people I have worked with during my time at ComNets, in the CRC 637 and at CIT, especially to Markus Becker and to Henning Rekersbrink.

Several students have also given me support as student assistants and by the work they did in their Diploma and Master Theses. As representatives for these students, David Bernau and Arturas Lukosius receive my thanks.

Last but not least, special thanks go to my friends, my parents, my sister, and my brother for all their mental support in the past years.

Bernd-Ludwig Wenning

Abstract

In communication networks as well as in logistic networks, methods to find an efficient path from a source to a destination are of major importance. In the former, data has to be transmitted from a sender to a receiver, while in the latter, goods have to be delivered from their origins to destinations. The methods to determine the paths through such networks are generally referred to as *routing methods*.

The topic of this thesis is positioned in this area of routing methods, more specifically in the area of routing based on current context. The routing approach developed in this thesis is applied to both application domains: *communication networks* and *logistic transportation networks*.

In both domains, there can be specific contexts or pieces of context information that influence the choice of routes. This thesis presents a novel routing approach with a generic formulation for context-based multi-criteria routing, which includes the routing message exchange concept as well as the decision function used to select routes. The generic formulation is then specialised for the two mentioned application domains, resulting in the Distributed Logistic Routing Protocol (DLRP) on the logistic side and the Reactive Environmental Monitoring Aware Routing (Reactive EMA) for wireless sensor networks on the communication networks side. In the core of both protocols, the Multi Criteria Context-based Decision (MCCD) system is applied, which is a major aspect of this thesis.

Analytical investigations on the volume of messaging that is generated by the routing protocol are presented. These investigations show the need for methods to prevent heavy routing message flooding. A combination of two flood limiting methods is proposed: The use of fixed hop limits plus the discarding of routing messages based on intermediate route evaluations. It is shown that these methods have a high potential to reduce the routing traffic.

For evaluation of the routing protocols, simulations were run in both domains and the results are presented. In the logistic domain, a topology based on a map of Germany with major cities and highway connections between them is used as evaluation scenario. The routing algorithm shows good performance within the scenario, especially with respect to vehicle utilisation and travelled distances. The routing traffic reduction introduced in the analytical part is also proven in the logistic simulation.

In the wireless sensor network domain, a scenario is used where the sensor nodes are threatened to be destroyed by the phenomenon they sense, which is a fire in the investigated scenario. As the sensors are supposed to monitor temperature, they can detect the fire but eventually get destroyed and therefore can neither sense nor relay any data afterwards. Reactive EMA is designed to consider this during the route selection, so that high temperature nodes are avoided as relay nodes, thus increasing the route reliability. For evaluation, Reactive EMA is compared to a proactive variant (Proactive EMA) and to the conventional AODV and OLSR routing protocols. In comparison to AODV and OLSR, Reactive EMA shows advantages, while Proactive EMA achieves comparable or better performance in some aspects.

Kurzfassung

Sowohl in Kommunikationsnetzen als auch in logistischen Netzen sind Verfahren zur Suche eines effizienten Wegs von einer Quelle zu einer Senke von großer Bedeutung. In Ersteren sind Daten von einem Sender zu einem Empfänger zu übertragen, in Letzteren sind Güter von Ursprungsorten zu ihren Zielorten zu transportieren. Die Verfahren zur Ermittlung der Wege durch solche Netze werden allgemein als *Routingverfahren* bezeichnet.

Das Thema dieser Dissertation ist im Bereich dieser Routingverfahren angesiedelt, spezifischer im Bereich des Routings auf Basis eines aktuellen Kontextes. Das in dieser Arbeit entwickelte Routingverfahren wird auf die folgenden beiden Anwendungsgebiete angewandt: *Kommunikationsnetze* und *transportlogistische Netze*.

In beiden Anwendungsdomänen können spezifische Kontexte oder Kontextinformationen existieren, die die Wahl der Routen beeinflussen. Diese Dissertation stellt einen neuen Routingansatz vor, der eine allgemeine Formulierung für kontextbasiertes, multikriterielles Routing beinhaltet. Diese Formulierung umfasst sowohl das Konzept des Austauschs von Routingpaketen als auch die für die Routenwahl verwendete Entscheidungsfunktion. Dieser allgemeine Ansatz wird für beide Anwendungsgebiete konkretisiert und resultiert dort im *Distributed Logistic Routing Protocol* (DLRP) auf Seiten der logistischen Netze und im *Reactive Environmental Monitoring Aware routing* (Reactive EMA) für drahtlose Sensornetze als Untermenge der Kommunikationsnetze. In beiden Protokollen wird die *Multi Criteria Context-based Decision function* (MCCD), die ein wesentlicher Teil dieser Arbeit ist, eingesetzt.

Der analytische Teil dieser Dissertation beinhaltet Untersuchungen zum durch das Routingprotokoll erzeugten Kommunikationsvolumen. Diese Untersuchungen zeigen die Notwendigkeit von Methoden zur Vermeidung großer routinginduzierter Kommunikationsvolumina auf. Eine Kombination zweier Methoden wird vorgeschlagen: Die Verwendung von festen Hop Limits und das Verwerfen von Routingnachrichten auf der Basis von Zwischenbewertungen der Route. Es wird gezeigt, dass diese Methoden ein großes Potential zur Beschränkung des Kommunikationsvolumens aufweisen.

Zur Bewertung der Routingprotokolle wurden für beide Anwendungsdomänen Simulationen durchgeführt, deren Resultate in dieser Arbeit präsentiert werden. In der Transportlogistik wurde eine Topologie verwendet, die auf einer Deutschlandkarte mit Großstädten und Autobahnverbindungen dazwischen basiert. Der vorgestellte Routingalgorithmus führt in diesem Szenario zu guten Ergebnissen, insbesondere in Bezug auf die Auslastung der Fahrzeuge und die gefahrenen Entfernungen. Darüber hinaus wird die Methode der Beschränkung des routinginduzierten Kommunikationsvolumens ebenfalls durch Resultate der Logistiksimulation positiv validiert.

Im Bereich der drahtlosen Sensornetze wird ein Szenario verwendet, in dem die Sensoren durch das Phänomen, das sie wahrnehmen, zerstört werden. Im verwendeten Szenario ist dieses Phänomen ein Feuer. Die Sensoren überwachen die Temperatur, daher können sie das Feuer wahrnehmen. Sie werden dann aber bald zerstört und können danach weder messen noch Daten weiterleiten. Reactive EMA berücksichtigt dies bei der Routenwahl, so dass vermieden wird, Sensorknoten, die einer hohen Temperatur ausgesetzt sind, als Weiterleitungsknoten in Routen zu verwenden. Zur Bewertung wird das Reactive EMA mit einer proaktiven Variante (Proactive EMA) und den konventionellen Protokollen AODV und OLSR verglichen. Im Vergleich zu AODV und OLSR hat Reactive EMA klare Vorteile, während Proactive EMA im Vergleich zu Reactive EMA in einigen Aspekten gleich gute oder bessere Leistung zeigt.

Contents

List of Figures

List of Tables

List of Abbreviations

AODV	Ad-hoc On-demand Distance Vector
APTEEN	Adaptive Periodic Threshold-sensitive Energy-Efficient sensor Network protocol
ASC	Aspect-Scale Context
BGP	Border Gateway Protocol
CAR	Context-Aware Routing protocol
cdf	Cumulative distribution function
C^2E^2S	Cluster and Chain based Energy*delay Efficient routing Scheme
CNCL	Communication Networks Class Library
CoOL	Context Ontology Language
CVRP	Capacitated Vehicle Routing Problem
DLRP	Distributed Logistic Routing Protocol
DSDV	Destination-Sequenced Distance Vector
DSR	Dynamic Source Routing
DYMO	Dynamic MANET On-demand routing
EGP	Exterior Gateway Protocol

EM-GMR	Energy and Mobility-aware Geographical Multipath Routing
EMA	Environmental Monitoring Aware routing
GMR	Geographical Multipath Routing
GPS	Global Positioning System
HEED	Hybrid Energy-Efficient Distributed routing
ID	Identifier
IEEE	Institute of Electrical and Electronics Engineers
IGP	Interior Gateway Protocol
LAN	Local Area Network
LEACH	Low-Energy Adaptive Clustering Hierarchy
LEACH-C	Centralised LEACH
LSP	Logistic Service Provider
LoCoSim	Logistics and Communication Simulator
MANET	Mobile Ad-hoc Network
MCCD	Multi-Criteria Context-based Decision
MCP	Multi-Constrained Path
MCR	Multi-Criteria Routing protocol
MTSP	Multiple Traveling Salesman Problem
mu	monetary units

NWAUF	Normalized Weighted Additive Utility Function	**SCAR**	Sensor Context-Aware Routing protocol
OLSR	Optimized Link-State Routing	**SINR**	Signal to Interference and Noise Ratio
OSPF	Open Shortest Path First		
OWL	Ontology Web Language	**SPIN**	Sensor Protocol for Information via Negotiation
PAN	Personal Area Network		
PDP	Pickup and Delivery Problem	**TDMA**	Time Division Multiple Access
PDPTW	Pickup and Delivery Problem with Time Windows	**TEEN**	Threshold-sensitive Energy-Efficient sensor Network protocol
PEGASIS	Power-Efficient Gathering in Sensor Information Systems	**TSP**	Traveling Salesman Problem
RDF	Resource Description Framework	**tu**	time units
RIP	Route Information Protocol	**VRP**	Vehicle Routing Problem
RN	Route Notification	**VRPTW**	Vehicle Routing Problem with Time Windows
RREQ	Route REQuest		
RSSI	Received Signal Strength Indicator	**WSN**	Wireless Sensor Network
		XML	eXtensible Markup Language

List of Symbols

Symbol	Area	See Page	Meaning
a_j	NWAUF	46	route alternative corresponds to j in the context notation
C_i	Context notation	23	context criterion i
C_{Prob}	HEED	13	preset cluster head percentage
CH_{Prob}	HEED	13	probability to become a cluster head
c	McCarthy context logic	19	(inner) context within McCarthy's context logic
c'	McCarthy context logic	19	outer context within McCarthy's context logic
c_i	Context notation	23	current value of C_i, according to S_i
$c_{i,j}$	MCCD	52	value of c_i for decision alternative j
$c_{i,min}$	Context notation	23	minimum possible value of C_i
$c_{i,max}$	Context notation	23	maximum possible value of C_i
$D_{Prop,l}$	Routing traffic analysis	69	Route request propagation depth on a path of length l
d_{route}	MCCD example	55	Delay on route
E_{max}	HEED	13	maximum energy of a node
$E_{residual}$	HEED	13	remaining energy of a node
E_{route}	MCCD example	55	Energy consumption on route
$f_{i,j}$	NWAUF	46	current value of criterion i for route alternative a_j corresponds to $c_{i,j}$ in the context notation/MCCD
$f'_{i,j}$	NWAUF	46	normalised value of criterion i for route alternative a_j

Symbol	Area	See Page	Meaning
$f_{i,min}$	NWAUF	46	minimum value for criterion i corresponds to $c_{i,min}$ in the context notation
$f_{i,max}$	NWAUF	46	maximum value for criterion i corresponds to $c_{i,max}$ in the context notation
$f_{s,i}(c_i)$	Context notation	23	scaling function for values c_i, $f_{s,i}$ is a specialisation of I_i
G	LEACH	12	Group of nodes not having served as cluster head in the last $1/P$ time intervals
G	MCCD example	55	Node group membership
$I_i(c_i)$	Context notation	23	context interpretation rule for value c_i of criterion C_i
$ist(c,s)$	McCarthy context logic	19	McCarthy's context logic: statement s is true in context c
j	Context notation	23	decision alternative
K	Routing traffic analysis	59	Number of edges at a node (node degree)
k	C^2E^2S	48	Maximum hop distance to cluster head
$\mathbf{L}$	Routing traffic analysis	69	Set of route forwarding limits
l	Routing traffic analysis	60	Route length
l_{max}	Routing traffic analysis	62	Maximum path length
N	Routing traffic analysis	59	Number of nodes in a network
n	LEACH	12	Node ID
$n_{notinc,l}$	Routing traffic analysis	61	Number of links in a path of length l that are not included in shorter paths
$n^*_{notinc,l}$	Routing traffic analysis	68	Number of links in a path of length l that are not included in shorter paths when using route request hop limits
n_{paths}	Routing traffic analysis	58	Number of paths between two nodes
n_{RREQs}	Routing traffic analysis	59	Number of route requests being sent in one route discovery

Symbol	Area	See Page	Meaning
P	LEACH	12	Target percentage of cluster heads
$P_{inc,m}$	Routing traffic analysis	61	Probability that a subpath of length m from a path of length l is included in paths with a length shorter than l
P_{link}	Routing traffic analysis	60	Link existence probability
P_{path}	Routing traffic analysis	60	Path existence probability
$P_{valid.l}$	Routing traffic analysis	69	Validity probability for a path of length l
p	C^2E^2S	48	optimal probability to become a cluster head
r	C^2E^2S	48	communication range
r	LEACH	12	Cluster head selection round
S_i	Context notation	23	scale (unit) in which C_i values should be given
s	McCarthy context logic	19	statement within McCarthy's context logic
$T(n)$	LEACH	12	Threshold for cluster head selection
T_C	APTEEN	13	Time count
$U(a_j)$	NWAUF	46	Normalized Weighted Additive Utility Function for route alternative a_j corresponds to U_j in the context notation
U_j	Context notation	23	combined utility for decision alternative j
U'_j	MCCD	52	Utility for decision alternative j, based on sum of logarithms
V_{FWD}	Routing traffic analysis	69	Validity function for route request forwarding
w_i	NWAUF, MCCD	46, 52	weight for criterion i
λ	C^2E^2S	48	sensor network density

1 Introduction

Routing is a major issue in all kinds of networks where items have to be transported from one location to another. These items can be, for example, pieces of information in communication networks or physical goods in logistic networks.

In communication networks, routing is usually a distributed task handled by several network nodes, either dedicated ones (routers) or any network participants in case of ad-hoc networks. In contrast to that, in logistic networks, routing traditionally is done by a central dispatcher who assigns routes and goods to vehicles. Recent developments in logistic research introduce a change from this central routing paradigm towards new routing solutions that are based on distributed information and decisions. Here, the routing challenges can be considered similar to those in communication networks, although there are differences between these networks, especially communication networks do not contain an equivalent to vehicles.

The "context" of an item is describing information on the item itself and its environment, i.e. it describes the situation the item is currently in. In communication networks, context can be, e.g. location, energy, connectivity, etc. In logistic networks, examples for context are time constraints, costs, available transport demand etc. If the network is dynamic, the context can vary dynamically, for example due to node mobility in communication networks and variable road congestion in logistics.

Context-based routing is already a research area within communication networks, especially in mobile ad-hoc networks and sensor networks. However, in most of the cases, the handling of context information is limited to the consideration of energy (energy-aware routing) or location (geographic routing).

As the transition from central dispatching to distributed routing in logistic networks is a radical paradigm shift, the state of the art is very limited here. Especially considering contextual information into the distributed routing process has not been covered before.

The routing concept developed in this thesis takes several aspects of context into account. Therefore, the route selection depends on multiple parameters and requires finding an overall optimum regarding the current context and the current route decision preferences. This means the parameters have to be combined into a multi-dimensional cost function. This cost function is applied both to routing in logistic networks and to routing in wireless sensor networks, using network-specific context criteria. Furthermore, it is shown that the cost function can also be applied for reduction of the solution space for route options, which reduces the communication that is required for the retrieval of routes.

1.1 Autonomous Cooperating Logistic Processes

As mentioned, one of the application areas covered in this thesis are logistic networks. Traditionally, routing in logistics is performed by central instances, either fleet management systems or even human dispatchers that optimise the vehicle routes based on the available information about the transport demand.

Recent developments in this area show an increasing complexity of these logistic optimisation problems. Online shopping causes an increasing demand for transportation of small pieces of goods on the consumer markets, just-in-time processes cause tight time constraints in transportation between production facilities, and so on. This increase in complexity makes central control of logistic processes more difficult. On the other side, the advances in information and communication technology enable local intelligence and decision-making on the individual logistic entities (goods, vehicles). Therefore, new paradigms in logistics are worth being investigated. To investigate the potentials of autonomy and distributed decision-making in logistics, the Collaborative Research Centre 637 (CRC 637) "Autonomous Cooperating Logistic Processes - A Paradigm Shift and its Limitations" was established at the University of Bremen in 2004 [SRWF04]. This CRC covers a wide range of aspects within the logistic processes that includes for example sensory aspects such as quality monitoring of goods, material flow topics such as goods and vehicle routing, and economic issues such as investigations on the consequences of autonomy for the management of logistic service providers. The term "Autonomous Control" is defined within the scope of this CRC as:

"Autonomous Control describes processes of decentralized decision-making in heterarchical structures. It presumes interacting elements in non-deterministic systems, which possess the capability and possibility to render decisions independently. The objective of Autonomous Control is the achievement of increased robustness and positive emergence of the total system due to distributed and flexible coping with dynamics and complexity." [WBP05]

The paradigm of Autonomous Cooperating Logistic Processes introduces autonomous control into all parts of the logistic processes. On the level of material flow, this means the individual entities such as goods and vehicles become autonomous. In order to achieve this autonomy, they have to become intelligent and able to communicate with other entities. Through the use of modern communication and information technology such as mobile communication networks and devices, embedded computers, wireless sensors, intelligent and mobile software agents, etc., this autonomy is implemented. This enables the logistic entities to individually make decisions on their routes.

These route decisions of intelligent, autonomous logistic entities are the target of the investigations in those parts of this thesis that cover the application of context-based routing in logistic networks. This research is part of the work in subproject "B1 - Autonomously Controlled Routing in Transport Networks", which is part of the aforementioned CRC.

1.2 Thesis Structure

The thesis is structured as follows:

Chapter 2 gives an overview on routing in logistic networks and in communication networks, the latter one with a special focus on wireless sensor networks. Based on this state of the art overview, the research focus of this thesis is identified within the area of context-based routing.

Chapter 3 first introduces a formalisation of context-based routing. Existing formalisation approaches are compared, before giving a formal definition of context and context-based routing that is used throughout this thesis. Then, a requirements analysis is done and based upon that, a generic protocol for context-based routing is designed. Decision systems that are of interest for this thesis are introduced in chapter 4. First, a state of the art overview on multi-criteria optimisation approaches in routing is given, then the multi-criterial approach used in this thesis is introduced as a result of the requirements on the decision system.

As a special analytic topic, the route discovery traffic is handled in chapter 5. Estimates on the amount of traffic are made and a way to reduce this traffic is proposed.

The protocol and the evaluation functions are evaluated in chapters 6 and 7, from which the former contains the evaluation in logistic networks, and the latter covers the evaluation in wireless sensor networks. The thesis finishes with chapter 8, where a conclusion is drawn and an outlook to possible enhancements is presented.

2 State of the Art

This chapter gives an overview over the state of the art concerning routing in communication networks and logistic networks. On the communication networks side, a special focus is on wireless sensor networks, as these are of interest for this thesis. Mobile ad-hoc network (MANET) protocols are also introduced as some ideas and concepts from them have a significant influence on the context-aware routing framework that is introduced in this thesis.

As one of the major focuses within this thesis is on multi-criteria route decisions, a separate state of the art overview specifically on multi-criteria routing is given in chapter 4. Protocols belonging to this category are therefore not presented here but in the later chapter.

In communication networks, the utilised routing mechanisms strongly depend upon the type of network that is used. On one hand, there are infrastructure-based networks, on the other hand, there are networks without fixed infrastructure components, so-called ad-hoc networks. In both categories, networks can be wired or wireless, although in most cases, ad-hoc networks are considered to be wireless.

In infrastructure networks, routing is usually done in dedicated infrastructure components, the *routers*. Their responsibility is to keep track of the network status and enable attached nodes to communicate with others. Usually, the topology of an infrastructure-based network is not very dynamic, so the routing information in that type of network can be valid for a long time.

Large-scale infrastructure networks often consist of several subnetworks which are interconnected through router-to-router connections. There can also be several levels of hierarchy within communication networks. In this case, the routers are also informing each other about gateways between the hierarchy levels. At different levels of the hierarchy, different routing methods may be used.

Basically, routing protocols in infrastructure-based networks are divided into Interior Gateway Protocols (IGP) and Exterior Gateway Protocols (EGP), depending on whether they route within one network or between networks. The most prominent IGPs are RIP (Routing Information Protocol) [Mal98] and OSPF (Open Shortest Path First) [Moy98]. As EGP, the BGP (Border Gateway Protocol)

[RLH06] is most widely used and can be considered as the "quasi-standard" routing protocol in the Internet.

Ad-hoc networks have no infrastructure components that can control the network, so the routing task has to be distributed among the network participants. Each node participating in the network is required to contribute to the discovery and maintenance of routes. Furthermore, the topology of wireless ad-hoc networks can be dynamic as wireless nodes can be moving. This implies that the routing mechanisms in wireless ad-hoc networks have to be able to react quickly to topology changes. Some of the well-known routing algorithms for mobile wireless ad-hoc networks are are introduced in the following section.

2.1 Routing in Mobile Ad-hoc Networks

Routing protocols in ad-hoc networks can mostly be classified into two main categories, proactive and reactive protocols, depending on whether they constantly maintain routing tables or discover routes on demand. A third category are the hybrid protocols which combine advantages of proactive and reactive protocols.

Proactive protocols are usually table driven. They constantly track the changes of the network topology and update their routing tables accordingly. To achieve this, there has to be a regular message pattern to keep track of the connectivity (keep-alive or hello messages), and if a node detects a change, routing table updates are multicasted or broadcasted to the neighbour nodes. This has the advantage that each node in the network always has up to date information about the available routes, but the drawback is that, especially in a highly dynamic network, frequent route updates may cause significant signalling overhead. Prominent examples for proactive protocols are DSDV (Destination Sequenced Distance Vector) [PB94] and OLSR (Optimized Link State Routing) [CJ03].

OLSR is explained here in more detail as it is also used in chapter 7. The route discovery and maintenance in OLSR is based on two types of messages: *HELLO* messages and *Topology Control (TC)* messages. Each node transmits HELLO messages at a fixed time interval. These messages contain addresses of all neighbour nodes that are locally known, based on previously received HELLO messages. So by the reception of HELLO messages, the network nodes obtain and update knowledge about their 1-hop and 2-hop neighbourhood. These messages are not forwarded to other nodes. Among the 1-hop neighbours, a node selects a set of MPR nodes (Multipoint Relay nodes) so that each 2-hop neighbour can be reached over at least one MPR node. These MPR nodes are used to forward broadcast messages. TC messages are also sent regularly. These messages are used to disseminate a node's neighbourhood information to the entire network, so the TC messages are forwarded by other nodes and thereby flooded into the network. The minimum neighbourhood information they have to contain is the node's MPR relations. Once a node has all topology information, it determines the routes with the help of a shortest-path algorithm such as Dijkstra's algorithm [Dij59].

Reactive protocols only determine routes when they are required, therefore, they are also called on-demand routing protocols. When a node needs to communicate in a network where a reactive protocol is used, it initiates the route discovery by sending out a "route request" message. This message is forwarded through the network from node to node until the communication partner is found. From there, a "route reply" message is sent back, informing the originator about the available route. The advantage of reactive routing is that signalling is only needed when a route has to be found, the drawback is that the route discovery process leads to a delay when a communication link is being established. In the area of reactive routing, there are several protocols available. The best known are DSR (Dynamic Source Routing) [JM96] and AODV (Ad-Hoc On-Demand Distance Vector) [PBRD03], a newer one is DYMO (Dynamic MANET On-Demand Routing) [CP07]. Due to their relevance in this thesis, the protocols DSR and AODV are described in more detail.

DSR (Dynamic Source Routing) is a reactive source routing protocol. When a node in a DSR-enabled network requires a route to a destination, it broadcasts a route request into the network. This route request is received by all neighbour nodes within its communication range and contains source and destination address and a sequence number. Nodes that receive the request can re-broadcast it after adding their own address to it. In this way, the requests collect the addresses of all nodes on a route as they propagate through the network. Re-broadcasting, however, is only done if the node that received the request did not receive another request with the same source address and sequence number before and if its own address is not in the route request yet. When the destination receives the route request, it creates a route reply that is sent back to the source, either on an already known route, on the reverse route that it knows through the incoming route request, or piggybacked on a route request that is sent out in the reverse direction. Upon reception of the route reply, the source can send its data. Each data packet includes the complete route, so that intermediate nodes do not have to maintain routing tables for forwarding the data. Route maintenance in DSR is done by hop-by-hop acknowledgements, either explicitly by sending these acknowledgements or implicitly by overhearing the transmission along the next hop. If the acknowledgement is missing, the node that expected to get this acknowledgement creates a route error message that is sent back to the source.

AODV (Ad-Hoc On-Demand Distance Vector) routing is similar to DSR when a route needs to be found. Here, the source also broadcasts a route request that is further propagated through the network by other nodes. Re-broadcasts are again only done if the node did not receive a route request from the same source with the same sequence number before. A difference is that the intermediate node addresses are not recorded in the route request when it propagates. Instead, the intermediate nodes create or update a reverse route entry in their local routing table. If the destination or a node that knows a route to the destination receives the route request, a route reply is created. This route reply is sent back to the source on the reverse path, according to the reverse route entries at the intermediate nodes. The intermediate nodes update their routing tables again when they forward a route reply, creating or updating a forward route entry. As all nodes have their routing tables, the source does not need to specify the route in each data packet that it sends when it has received the route reply. Routes in AODV have a limited lifetime and need to be maintained. This maintenance means the nodes have to keep track of their local connectivity. This can be done by explicit or implicit acknowledgements (as in DSR) and by the use of periodic hello messages. It should be noted that only nodes with an active route should transmit hello messages. When a route breakage is detected by missing hello messages or acknowledgements, the node that detects it can either initiate a local repair attempt or it creates a route error message that is sent to its precursors so that the upstream nodes know that a new route discovery is required.

Hybrid ad-hoc routing protocols are a combination of proactive and reactive routing protocols which combine some advantages of both. The ZRP (Zone Routing Protocol) [Haa97] divides the network into non-overlapping routing zones. Within a zone, routing is done proactively, while routing across multiple zones is done with a reactive approach. In this way, route discovery delays are avoided within the zone, while the signalling required to maintain routing tables is restricted to the zone, thus avoiding excessive route maintenance signalling.

2.2 Routing in Wireless Sensor Networks

A wireless sensor network is a special kind of ad-hoc network. It consists of a sometimes large amount of sensor nodes which have some limitations due to their size. The sensor nodes usually sense their environment and transmit their data to one or more sinks. So, generally speaking, the communication in wireless sensor networks is often a many-to-one or a many-to-few communication.

There are a couple of routing algorithms for wireless sensor networks, which according to [AKK04] can be categorised by their network structure as a) flat routing, b) hierarchical routing and c) location-based routing.

Flat routing means that sensor information is forwarded from node to node until it reaches the sink. No hierarchy of nodes is present here. Some examples for flat routing protocols are given in section 2.2.1.

Hierarchical routing is a type of routing where not all nodes are treated equally, but a node hierarchy is present. Nodes can for example be grouped together in a cluster, and a node which acts as a so-called cluster head receives the data from the other nodes in the cluster and forwards it in the direction of the sink. Examples for hierarchical routing protocols in wireless sensor networks are given in section 2.2.2.

Location-based routing takes location information into account when determining routes. Each node is aware of its geographical position (e.g. by the use of GPS), and this knowledge is exploited to create routes. Location-based routing can be considered as a special case of context-aware routing, with the location being the context information that is used. Therefore, the categorisation given in [AKK04] can be modified to label the third category as context-aware routing.

Generally, if a routing algorithm is context-aware, this does not mean that it is not flat or hierarchical. In fact, it can be either of those. For example, an algorithm that contains a location-based clustering method, performs a hierarchical routing that utilises the context information about the nodes' locations. If no cluster formation is present in the context-aware routing algorithm, the routing can be regarded as flat context-aware routing.

2.2.1 Flat Routing in Wireless Sensor Networks

In flat routing protocols, all nodes have equal functions and responsibilities. Flat routing protocols have several similarities to routing protocols in wireless ad-hoc networks. The routes established in a wireless sensor network with flat routing are usually multi-hop routes that are optimised with respect to energy efficiency or other constraints. As the sensor networks can be large, the assignment of global identifiers to the nodes may not be feasible. Therefore, flat routing protocols in wireless sensor networks are often data-centric, i.e. they rely on data collection and dissemination in the nodes' vicinity rather than establishing routes between specific endpoints.

The simplest solution to flat routing in wireless sensor networks is flooding, where the nodes simply broadcast the information they have to all nodes within communication range. This, however, is not efficient as there can be a high volume of redundant traffic in case of overlapping sensing areas or multiple communication paths for one single message. Therefore, these issues have to be addressed in the routing protocols.

One example of a flat routing protocol is *Directed Diffusion* [IGE00]. In Directed Diffusion, a sink (i.e. a base station) announces interest for specific sensor data to the network. As this interest announcement propagates, it defines gradients for the message flow between the sensor nodes. When nodes have data that correspond to the interest, this data is sent to the sink along routes that result from the gradients. Figure 2.1 illustrates this.

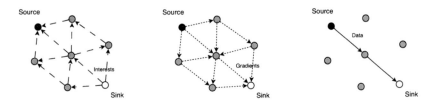

Figure 2.1: Directed Diffusion [IGE00]

Directed Diffusion can therefore be labelled as a polling-based flat routing, as the sink is polling the data from the network, and the nodes remain silent if there is no current interest for data. This is beneficial in cases where sensor data is only requested in varying infrequent intervals, as there is only on-demand communication when there is interest for sensor data.

A group of flat routing protocols is the *Sensor Protocol for Information via Negotiation* (SPIN) family [HKB99][KHB02]. Compared to the Directed Diffusion described before, SPIN starts at the other end of the sensor data flow: at the source. It is not a pure polling-based routing but based on a combination of advertisements and polling. If a source has something to send, it announces to its neighbour nodes that it has data. The neighbour nodes can respond with a request for the data or ignore the advertisement. Then, the source sends the data to those who have requested it. Nodes that have received the data can now combine it with own data or just provide it to further parts of the network using the same advertisement mechanism. However, they are not sending advertisements back to the originator of the data as it is known that the data is already present there. The message flow is illustrated in Figure 2.2: Node A has data to send and advertises it to node B. Node B replies with a request, upon which A sends the data. B then again advertises the data to its neighbours, receives requests and transmits the data.

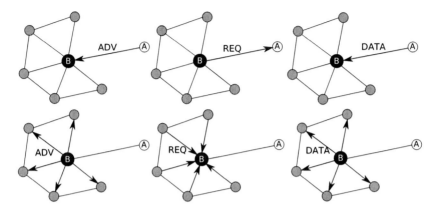

Figure 2.2: Message flow in SPIN [KHB02]

It has to be noted that the operation of this protocol is based on the assumption that nodes always have interest in data that they do not possess yet. This means they should only ignore advertisements if the advertised data is already known. Otherwise, it may happen that sinks do not get any data because intermediate nodes are not interested in the advertised data.

2.2.2 Hierarchical Routing in Wireless Sensor Networks

Hierarchical routing protocols introduce a hierarchy into the network, either by grouping the network nodes into so-called clusters or by establishing trees.

In cluster-based hierarchical protocols, each cluster has a cluster head that acts as a communication relay for the other cluster members. The main difference among the cluster-based algorithms is how the clusters are formed. The simplest approach is *Static Clustering*. Static Clustering is not a specific algorithm or protocol, but it stands for any method of defining static clusters and assigning static cluster heads in the network. Here, the clusters are defined when the network is set up, and they are not changed during the network's lifetime. The cluster heads are usually chosen according to an optimisation target such as network lifetime or connectivity. As the cluster heads consume more energy than the other network nodes, they should be equipped with a stronger power supply. If not, they become the weak points in the network: When their energy resources are depleted, the corresponding clusters drop out of the network even if most of the cluster members still have energy resources left which would enable them to continue operation.

A more advanced cluster-based approach is the *Low-Energy Adaptive Cluster-ing Hierarchy* (LEACH) [HCB00]. In LEACH, a self-organising clustering with randomised cluster head rotation is used in the network. The cluster heads in LEACH are more than just message relays: they also perform data aggregation to reduce the redundancy of communication in the network. The rotation of cluster head selection is repeated in regular time intervals. Each node is choosing to be a cluster head by selection of a random number out of a uniform distribution in the interval $[0..1]$. If the number is below a threshold $T(n)$, the node becomes a cluster head in the current time interval (the current round). The threshold is defined as:

$$
T(n) = \begin{cases} \dfrac{P}{1 - P * (r \bmod \frac{1}{P})} & \text{if } n \in G \\ 0 & \text{otherwise} \end{cases} \tag{2.1}
$$

Here, n is the node id, P is the target percentage of cluster heads, G is the group of nodes not having served as a cluster head in the last $\frac{1}{P}$ time intervals, and r is the current round. The result of this randomised cluster head rotation is an equal distribution of the cluster head responsibility among all nodes in the network. After having chosen to be a cluster head, the nodes announce their new status to their environment so that the surrounding nodes can select a cluster which is most suitable with regard to the energy required for communication. After the clusters have been established, the cluster head assigns TDMA time slots to the cluster members to minimise collisions within the cluster.

A variant of LEACH is LEACH-C, the centralised version of LEACH. In this variant, the cluster head selection is not performed autonomously on the network members but centrally on the base station by an optimisation over the complete network. The advantage of the centralised cluster head selection is that an optimum of cluster sizes and cluster head distribution can be assured. The drawback is that the base station needs to have knowledge of the complete network topology at any time, so a higher signalling overhead is required.

The *Threshold sensitive Energy-Efficient sensor Network protocol* (TEEN) [MA01] is based on the same cluster formation approach as LEACH-C. While the cluster formation is the same, the communication concept regarding the sensor data is different. Instead of using a TDMA cycle with time slots for each cluster member, the cluster head publishes two threshold values for sensed data: a "soft threshold" and a "hard threshold". The soft threshold defines a minimum differ-ence in the sensed value that triggers a transmission, the hard threshold defines an absolute value for the sensed data to trigger a transmission. As long as neither the soft threshold nor the hard threshold are exceeded, the cluster members remain silent, thus saving energy. As the authors of [MA01] state, the TEEN protocol is suitable for cases where fast alerting is critical in case of a specific event, while the protocol is less suitable for continuous monitoring tasks where sensor data has to be provided on a regular basis. Another drawback of TEEN is that, if the thresholds are never exceeded, the network may silently die without the user being able to notice.

To overcome these shortages of TEEN, an enhanced version was developed by the same authors: *Adaptive Periodic Threshold sensitive Energy-Efficient sensor Network protocol* (APTEEN) [MA02]. This protocol combines advantages of LEACH-C and TEEN. After cluster formation, a TDMA cycle *and* threshold values are published to the nodes, along with a time count value T_C. This time count defines an interval in which the nodes should periodically transmit their sensor data. It is supposed to be a multiple of the TDMA cycle length. Thereby, the frequency of regular transmissions can be controlled as a trade-off between energy-saving and up-to-date data. When a critical situation occurs (i.e. one of the threshold values is exceeded), a transmission is triggered irrespective of when the next regular transmission is scheduled. This enables APTEEN to quickly respond to critical situations. The time count and the threshold values in APTEEN have to be chosen according to the three target constraints reactivity, energy consumption and up-to-dateness of monitoring information.

Another cluster-based routing approach that is using energy consumption as its main criterion is the *Hybrid Energy-Efficient Distributed routing* (HEED) [YF04]. Similar to LEACH, the cluster head selection is done in a distributed fashion by nodes that decide to become a cluster head. The probability to become a cluster head in HEED is

$$CH_{Prob} = C_{Prob} \frac{E_{residual}}{E_{max}} \tag{2.2}$$

with C_{Prob} as a preset initial percentage of cluster heads in the network, $E_{residual}$ as the node's estimated remaining energy and E_{max} as the energy in case of fully charged batteries. According to the authors, the remaining energy does not have to be measured but can be calculated based on the sensing, computation and communication that the node has performed.

A cluster formation phase in HEED consists of several iterations. In each iteration, a HEED node that is "uncovered" (i.e. has not received any cluster head announcements from its surrounding) chooses to be a cluster head with probability CH_{Prob}. If it decides to become a cluster head, it sends out a cluster head announcement, either to be a tentative or a final cluster head. In case the node has not decided to become a cluster head but it is still uncovered, the process is repeated with doubled CH_{prob}. If CH_{prob} is 1, the node has no other choice than to become a cluster head, so it announces itself as a final cluster head. Covered

nodes and tentative cluster heads maintain a sorted list of cluster head announcements (including their own) from which they select their cluster head as the one
with the least cost.

A tree-based hierarchical routing protocol is *Power-Efficient Gathering in Sensor Information Systems* (PEGASIS) [LR02]. In PEGASIS, the network is partitioned into chains instead of clusters. These chains are generated either by the
nodes themselves or by the base station. If the nodes generate the chains, each
node is assumed to have full knowledge of the network, and the chains are created
by a greedy algorithm, starting from those nodes which are most distant from the
base station. Similar to LEACH, PEGASIS is also using time intervals (rounds).
In each round, exactly one node in a chain is selected as a leader node. This selection is done randomly so that all nodes in the chain will become a leader node
for some time. The message flow is now as follows: The leader node transmits
a token towards both ends of the chain, which is forwarded by the intermediate
nodes. Upon token reception, the endpoints of the chain are starting the communication by sending their data to the next neighbour in the chain. The neighbour
is then aggregating the received data with its own and forwards the data along the
chain towards the leader. When the leader has received the data from both ends of
the chain, it aggregates the data with its own and transmits to the base station (see
Figure 2.3).

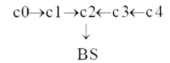

Figure 2.3: PEGASIS communication chain

According to [LR02], PEGASIS significantly outperforms LEACH in terms of
network lifetime in networks of different sizes and topologies.

An algorithm that combines chains and clusters by partitioning the network
into clusters and establishing chains of cluster heads for the communication between the clusters and the base station is presented in [HH06]. The approach is
named *Cluster and Chain based Energy*Delay Efficient Routing Scheme* (C^2E^2S).
The performance of this algorithm is compared to the above mentioned algorithms
LEACH-C, HEED and a hierarchical variant of PEGASIS. As the approach is also

taking multiple criteria into account, it is discussed in more detail in section 4.1 of this thesis.

The sensor network routing protocols that have been introduced here are all only considering one context parameter, in most cases this is the energy efficiency. Additionally, they are usually targeted for single-sink scenarios, and the route decision functions are fixed. Based on these shortcomings, the resulting research challenge for this thesis is identified in section 2.4.

2.3 Routing in Logistic Networks

The classical routing scenarios in logistic networks are different from those in communication networks: While there are several cooperating entities (routers) in communication networks, the usual logistic network has one central routing entity. When speaking of a logistic network, this normally means a network as seen from the perspective of a logistic service provider (LSP). The LSP has a fleet of vehicles and aims to fulfil the current set of orders with this fleet. This means doing an overall optimisation of the routes for all transport demands that are known. Dependent on the complexity of the LSP's optimisation scenario, the approaches to solve the optimisation task range from a human dispatcher who composes tours mainly based on experience, up to powerful computation servers that use heuristics to find an optimum.

Dependent on the goods flow scenarios, such as many sources to one destination (collection), one source to many destinations (distribution) or many sources to many destinations (pickup-and-delivery) and the number of available vehicles, different standard problems can be identified. Collection and distribution scenarios are the usual case on the "last mile" of logistic networks that use a hub-and-spoke concept, which is very common among large LSPs such as DHL or UPS. Pickup-and-delivery scenarios are more common for courier companies, for example.

Furthermore, logistic scenarios can be differentiated into static scenarios where all transport orders, travel times etc. are known in advance and are not changed, and dynamic scenarios where new orders can enter the scenario at any point of time, existing orders can be changed and so on.

2.3.1 Static Logistic Scenarios

The routing scenarios which have the longest history in logistics are static scenarios. They contain one or more mobile elements (vehicles) and a fixed set of orders or locations to be visited. The most prominent of these problems are the

Traveling Salesman Problem (TSP), the *Vehicle Routing Problem* (VRP) and the *Pickup-and-Delivery Problem* (PDP).

The original TSP is an optimisation problem with the goal of finding the shortest path for a round trip among a set of locations without visiting one location twice. Therefore, it is a pure sequencing problem. The TSP appears to have first been mentioned (although not as a mathematical problem) in an 1832 manual for travelling salespersons and was first treated as a mathematical optimisation problem by the mathematician Karl Menger in the late 1920s [Sch05]. It assumes that all locations have to be visited by the same salesperson, and no further constraints such as time windows or transport capacities are present in the original problem. A variant of the TSP is the *Multiple Traveling Salesman Problem* (MTSP), where the locations are to be visited in several round trips (according to the number of salespersons), where each of the round trips may be done by one salesperson. The MTSP can be transformed into an original TSP by inserting duplicate instances of the starting point into the set of locations to be visited.

In the VRP, a fleet of vehicles is to be used to visit the set of locations in round trips. So without any constraints, it is the same as a MTSP. The VRP was first formulated as "Truck Dispatching Problem" in [DR59]. In the VRP, the optimisation is twofold: Additionally to the sequencing, an optimised assignment of locations to the available vehicles is required in order to find a global optimum. Usually, the VRP is bound to constraints that make it different from the MTSP. One constraint that is already mentioned in the original VRP formulation is the vehicles' capacity. The capacity causes that only a subset of the MTSP solutions are feasible, as the other solutions may exceed the capacity of at least one of the vehicles. This special form of VRP is known under the term *Capacitated Vehicle Routing Problem* (CVRP). Another constrained VRP variant is the *Vehicle Routing Problem with Time Windows* (VRPTW) [Sol87]. In the VRPTW, time windows are specified for each location, denoting when this location should be visited.

The PDP has a substantial difference compared to the VRP and the TSP: The locations in the PDP always form source-destination pairs. This means the source and the destination have to be on the same route, thus forming a constraint for the assignment of locations to routes. The source-destination pairs also imply sequencing constraints as the source has to be visited before the sink, as goods obviously cannot be delivered before they were picked up. Moreover, there may be time windows defined for each pickup and each delivery, in which case the resulting task is labelled *Pickup and Delivery Problem with Time Windows* (PDPTW) [MM98].

As all these optimisation problems are of NP-hard computational complexity, they can usually not be solved exactly within acceptable time. Therefore, they are usually solved based on heuristic methods such as Genetic Algorithms ([BB04]), Tabu Search ([NB00]), Memetic Algorithms ([Sch04]) or others.

2.3.2 Routing in Dynamic Logistic Environments

In logistic scenarios with high dynamics such as randomly incoming new transport demand or varying travel times, it may not be sufficient to solve the global optimisation problem on an infrequent basis of several hours. Therefore, more responsive methods are applied here. Two main flavours of these methods are *rolling horizon planning* and *real-time decision making*.

Rolling horizon planning, as introduced by Psaraftis for the dynamic PDPTW [Psa88], is considered as the standard solution for dynamic optimisation problems. In this planning approach, there is a time horizon up to which the planning is optimised. After a fixed time interval has passed, the horizon is moved forward according to this interval and planning cycle is done for the time until the new horizon. This is continued with fixed inter-planning intervals. In each new cycle, the situational changes (e.g. new transport requests) that happened since the last cycle can be taken into account. The reactivity of rolling horizon planning is therefore limited by the planning intervals.

In real-time decision making [PMGB02], the solution that is currently executed is modified as soon as a significant change triggers a re-evaluation. Actually, the re-evaluation is again a heuristic approach with the constraint that the routes that are currently being served cause several solutions to become impossible. While real-time decision making can theoretically react immediately on situational changes, it is still limited in its reactivity as the computation time required for a re-evaluation cycle implies a lower limit for the interval between two re-evaluations.

2.3.3 Distributed Routing in Logistics

The reactivity limitations of the central planning approaches are the target of distributed routing approaches. Distributed routing in logistic networks is a new and completely different concept that is drawing interest in relation to the new paradigm of *Autonomous Cooperating Logistic Processes* [SRWF04] [SRFR⁺05]. The idea behind autonomous cooperation of logistic entities is to reduce the complexity of the routing tasks (and thus increase the reactivity) by having local decisions based on local knowledge instead of having global decisions in a central routing instance. The ongoing evolution in the development of hardware and software for computation and communication offers the possibility to equip logistic entities with devices capable of cooperation and autonomous decision making.

2.4 Research Challenge

In the current state of the art, context-based routing in wireless sensor networks is mostly limited to a few parameters with little adaptivity to special requirements. The use of context information such as location, energy etc. is usually handled in routing frameworks with a specific, fixed selection of parameters and their weights. Further, several routing methods in wireless sensor networks rely on the presence of only one sink in the network. If there are more sinks, different message flow directions might have to be realised within one network, which leads to new challenges for the algorithms. Some approaches to multi-criteria routing in wireless networks (partially not necessarily sensor networks) which have been published recently are discussed in more detail in section 4.1. However, these approaches also have their limitations as it is pointed out in that section.

In logistic networks, autonomous controlled routing as such is still in an early stage of development. Naturally, this also holds for context-based routing as a subset of autonomous controlled routing. As the move from centrally planned travelling schedules to autonomously acting entities is a fundamental paradigm shift, the benefits of autonomous cooperating logistic processes have to be identified and proven.

The research challenge in this thesis is to develop a new, generalised kind of context-based routing. The routing framework should be a lot more adaptive and flexible than current approaches that are bound to individual, limited application areas. Especially, the target functions for route optimisation and the corresponding parameters are supposed not to be fixed a-priori, but a generalised multi-criteria target function, the *Multi-Criteria Context-based Decision function* (MCCD), is to be developed. The context parameters should be specifiable during the route discovery process.

To evaluate the context-based routing concept, scenarios from transport logistics as well as scenarios from wireless sensor networks are chosen as application domains in which the routing concept is evaluated.

3 Context-based Routing Protocol Development

One of the goals of this thesis is to specify a generic routing protocol framework for context-aware routing in a dynamic environment. This chapter first presents a formal description and definition of the term "context-based routing" as it is used in the scope of this thesis. Then a requirements analysis for the specification and design of the protocol is done and the protocol that has been designed based upon the requirements is presented.

3.1 Formal Description of Context-based Routing

This section defines and formalises *context*, first by providing a look into the state of the art, and then by introducing the definition and terminology used throughout this thesis.

3.1.1 State of the Art in Formalisation

Formalisation of contextual information into logics was first introduced by McCarthy [McC87], further specified in follow-up publications such as [McC93]. According to McCarthy, statements are only true within a given context. His formalisation is based on a notion of the form:

$$c' : ist(c,s). \tag{3.1}$$

This denotes that the statement s is true within the context c, while this relation is used in another "outer context" c'. With some more relations of a similar structure and usual logical operators ($\land$, $\lor$, $\neg$ etc.), a framework is created which enables complex logical expressions based on those elementary relations. However, this context logic is limited to binary logic. A statement is either true or false with respect to a specific context. No continuous scale with respect to a context is used. Therefore, it is not applicable if more than just "true" and "false" is required to describe the context criterion value.

More recent approaches to formalise context information for the use in intelligent systems focus on the use of ontologies, especially by describing the context with the help of the Resource Description Framework (RDF, [Bec04]) or the Ontology Web Language (OWL, [MvH04]). These two description languages are not independent of each other, but OWL is based on RDF and extends it.

An ontology-based approach is the definition of the *Context Ontology Language* (CoOL) [SLPF03]. This language can be projected to OWL as well as to the logic language F-Logic. A so-called *Aspect-Scale-Context* (ASC) model is used to describe the context. Aspect here means the type of context, e.g. the distance to a reference point. The scale defines, as the name already states, how the information is scaled, e.g. in metres, kilometres or miles, and the valid range of values for the aspect. It is not limited to primitive data types as in the mentioned example, but it can also be an object consisting of several values, as it is required, e.g., for geographic coordinates. As it can easily be seen from the context example, an aspect may have several valid scales, and there must be mapping functions to map between the scales. The actual context is then the current value of the aspect along with information about the scale in use, and eventually some other information characterising the quality of the information, such as minimum error, mean error and a time stamp. Additionally, the model used in the CoOL defines "meta-context" which is context information that characterises the quality of other context information, thus being a kind of higher-order context.

3.1.2 Definition of Context

For a formalisation of context-based routing, a definition of context and context-awareness is required. A definition of context is given by Dey and Abowd:

"Context is any information that can be used to characterize the situation of an entity. An entity is a person, place or object that is considered relevant to the interaction between a user and an application, including the user and applications themselves." [DA99]

Within the scope of this thesis, the use of contextual information is not restricted to the the interaction between users and applications, but the interaction among the devices in a sensor network or among logistic entities is of special interest here. Therefore, the cited definition has to be adapted:

Context is any information that can be used to characterise the situation of an entity. An entity is a person, place or object that is considered relevant to the interaction between users, objects and applications, including the users, objects and applications themselves.

In wireless sensor networks, the term "context" refers to the situation and the environment of the sensor nodes, which are objects in the terminology of the given definition. This sensor node context can be, for example:

- location
- energy level
- connectivity
- sensed data
- individual preferences
- movement

"Context" in logistic networks can be the context of a vehicle or of a piece of goods. Examples are:

- location
- load status (loaded/unloaded)
- capacity/volume
- destination
- time constraints

Generally speaking, context can be, in the scope of this work, any information that can have impact on the routing process. Furthermore, the handling of contextual information often not only has to do with the values themselves (such as the geographical position, for example) but also with semantics, that means the correct interpretation of the given values. Therefore, the semantics can be regarded as an integral part of context information. A full description of a context criterion, including the semantics, comprises the following:

- information on what kind of context is described, e.g. "delay"
- information about the scale, e.g. seconds or milliseconds
- possible value range, e.g. $[0, \infty]$
- value interpretation rules, e.g. target values, fuzzy rules.

The description of a current context then at least consists of the description of all relevant criteria as defined above, as well as the current context values for all these criteria. Additionally, it can also contain rules for correct interpretation of the combined context.

Context-awareness means that the entity that is performing an action does this while taking into account its own current context and the context of those it is interacting with. In the scope of routing in dynamic networks, context-aware routing refers to routing methods that use context information such as those mentioned in the above examples to determine routes that fulfil requirements that depend on

the context and are specific for the application domain and the application context
(e.g. required reliability or speed).

3.1.3 Formalisation in this Thesis

The formalisation of context that is required in this thesis has to represent both the
syntax and the semantics of the represented context information (cf. section 3.2.1).

As wireless sensor networks are one possible application domain for the routing
framework developed here, the limited resources on wireless sensor nodes have to
be taken into account. This implies that it is not practically feasible (or at least not
efficient) to perform reasoning over a full-featured OWL ontology on the nodes.
Additionally, including such an ontology in the protocol messages would create a
significant overhead which is not reasonable in wireless sensor networks. Therefore, a lightweight formal description of context syntax and semantics is required
for the wireless sensor networks.

The constraints in logistic networks are different. When thinking about a communication and computation unit on a container, a truck or even in a distribution
centre, message size and required processing power are no strongly limiting factors. So, it is possible here to use the full power of ontology languages and corresponding reasoning engines.

Hence, depending on the application domain, the requirements on the representation of context semantics are different. As the objective of this thesis, however,
is not the creation of different solutions for different application domains but the
design of a unique flexible protocol that is applicable in the different domains, the
strictest constraints set the limits for the complexity.

3.1.3.1 Context Notation

The initial step for a formalisation is the definition of a context notation. The
notation defined here is to be used throughout this thesis for any expressions that
are developed or used for context description, handling and evaluation.

Table 3.1 lists the most important parts of the notation.

While the use and meaning of the first five rows in the table are quite obvious,
the remaining ones require some explanation. The symbol $I_i(c_i)$ is to be considered as a general term for context interpretation rules, including scaling functions,
mappings to fuzzy sets and so on. It is not limited to a specific method of context
interpretation.

The function $f_{s,i}(c_i)$ assumes that the context values are scaled by the use of a
function with criterion-specific characteristics. In that sense, it is a special case

symbol	meaning
C_i	context criterion i
S_i	scale (unit) in which C_i values should be given
c_i	current value of C_i, according to S_i
$c_{i,min}$	minimum possible value of C_i
$c_{i,max}$	maximum possible value of C_i
$I_i(c_i)$	context interpretation rule for value c_i of criterion C_i
$f_{s,i}(c_i)$	scaling function for values c_i
	$f_{s,i}$ is a specialisation of I_i which projects c_i to the interval [0 1]
	for details see section 4.2 and the following ones
U_j	combined utility for decision alternative j
	(i.e. evaluation result for j)
	determined based on all relevant context criteria

Table 3.1: Context notation

of a context interpretation rule $I_i(c_i)$. When combining several context values into one common metric, the scaling functions play an important role as they can be used to map the different value ranges of different criteria into a common value range, thus preventing the dominance of single criteria with value ranges that are extremely high or low compared to the other criteria values. The importance of these scaling functions is represented in this work through detailed discussions in the chapters 4 and 6.

The combined utility U_j is used for the evaluation of decision alternatives (i.e. routes). It is determined based on a combination of all relevant context criteria. To achieve a reasonable evaluation, the aforementioned scaling functions should be applied to the context values before combining them into the utility. In section 4.2, U_j is further specified to be the weighted multiplication of all relevant $f_{s,i}(c_i)$.

3.2 Requirement Analysis

As the intended use of the routing protocol framework is neither restricted to a specific use case nor to a specific environment, a high flexibility is needed. This refers to the relevant context parameters as well as to the decision system that is used to select routes. The decision systems are covered in detail in chapter 4, so in the current chapter, the focus is on the specification of message formats and message flows. All entities participating in the routing process are considered as being able to do parts of the decisions that are required.

3.2.1 Information to be Carried

The intended flexibility implies that the context information that is used in the protocol is not restricted to a specific set of parameters. Therefore, the message format must represent this, i.e. it has to provide the possibility to include virtually every kind of (measurable) context parameter. The recipient of such a message has to obtain:

- knowledge about what kind of parameter is included (syntax and semantics)
- the context parameter's value
- rules how to handle the parameter.

For a routing scheme that is based on multiple criteria, each of these criteria that is used in the decision process is different. This means that at least the first two of the three items mentioned above have to be present individually for each context criterion.

Concerning the information about syntax and semantics, for which the term meta-informa-tion is used from here on, there are different possible ways to include this information in the messages:

- explicit inclusion of meta-information in the message
- a reference to an entry in a common knowledge base (e.g. a context ID)
- a reference to a "location" where the information can be obtained (e.g. a web link to an ontology document).

Including only a reference to the meta-information in the messages has the advantage that it reduces the message size, but it implies other challenges:

If the reference points to a location like a web link, this link must be reachable by the recipient of the message. Depending on the application domain, this may or may not work. In communication networks, it will most likely not work as a running route discovery usually means that some communication routes are not available yet, but a communication route to the link destination would be needed. Additionally, the retrieval of meta-information from the linked location creates additional communication overhead, especially if the nodes do not or only temporarily cache the meta-information.

Consequently, the reference to a location is not a usable option in communication networks, especially due to the reachability issue. In logistic networks, it would theoretically be possible, but the additional communication overhead remains. Furthermore, a central meta-information repository which is accessible for all participating entities would be a potentially weak point in a distributed routing scenario: It introduces a single point of failure. Even worse, if a malicious attack is conducted where the meta-information is altered, the entire logistic network may cease to function properly.

In case the reference is a kind of context ID which is mapped to the meta-information through a common knowledge base, the challenge arises how to establish and maintain this knowledge base. Two options are theoretically possible: a dedicated network node which maintains the knowledge base and is known by all network nodes or a distributed knowledge base. The first option has the same problems as the previously discussed reference to an external location: reachability by the other network nodes cannot generally be assumed. The dedicated node would be a single point of failure in this scenario and a potential target for attacks.

That leaves the option of a distributed knowledge base as the more robust solution. This option, however, implies that the distributed knowledge has to be kept up-to-date. Therefore, an update mechanism is required that takes care of this. This mechanism requires a push-mode as well as a pull-mode and will be part of the protocol specification.

A combination of using a common knowledge base and including meta-information in the routing messages can also be possible as a trade-off between required message size and knowledge base maintenance. This combination can be that some frequently used context parameters and their handling are well-known to the nodes and do not require meta-information in the routing messages, while other parameters need to be transmitted with detailed meta-information about how they should be treated.

Apart from the pure specification of context, the individual node in the network also needs to know what it has to do with it. It needs knowledge about what own context information it has to add and whether it has to forward the message, for example. This thesis proposes that the decision whether to forward the message is based partly on the evaluation of context criteria. This proposal is discussed in more detail in Chapter 5.

Consequently, the general structure of context information in a routing message can be specified as depicted in figure 3.1.

Depending on the application area, the specified fields can be subdivided into several substructures (see 3.3.2.1 and 3.3.3.1). In routing schemes where only the next hop is of interest, this information structure is sufficient, but in routing schemes where the exact route is to be known at the sender (e.g. source routing schemes), the route hops have to be specified additionally.

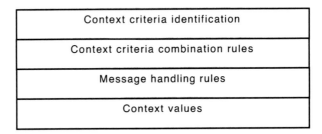

| Context criteria identification |
| Context criteria combination rules |
| Message handling rules |
| Context values |

Figure 3.1: General context information structure

3.2.2 Message Flows

Distributed routing methods, which are currently mainly used in ad-hoc communication networks, can be categorised into proactive and reactive methods (see Chapter 2). Depending on which of these options is chosen, the message flows are different.

3.2.2.1 Message Flows in Proactive Routing

In proactive routing protocols, the participating nodes maintain route tables which either contain complete routes to the known destinations or at least information about the next hop towards a destination. These tables have to be kept up to date constantly. To assure this, these protocols need at least a kind of "keep-alive" signalling to ensure that there are no undetected node or connection failures. Furthermore, if a node detects a change in the network (e.g. a neighbour node fails, not sending keep-alive signals any more), the information about the change has to be communicated to the other nodes in the network, which means broadcasting an update message to the surrounding neighbour nodes. The neighbour nodes then again have to rebroadcast update messages if the received updates are relevant for them.

3.2.2.2 Message Flows in Reactive Routing

In reactive routing protocols, the classical concept of route discovery is the use of *route request* and *route reply* messages. The source that needs a route sends out a route request to its neighbour nodes, usually by broadcasting the request. The neighbour nodes eventually add data to the request and forward it to their neighbours. In this way, the network is flooded with route requests. In order to limit the flood, hop limits or timeouts are used. When those limits are reached, the requests are not forwarded further. Additionally, protocols such as AODV, which are using sequence numbers in their route requests, only forward the first incoming route request of a route discovery. Later incoming requests related to the same route discovery (identified by having the same sequence number) are discarded. When the route request is received by either a node knowing a route to the destination or by the destination itself, a route reply message is created and sent back to the source, usually by travelling backwards on the same path through which the request came.

3.2.2.3 Consequences for a Context-aware Routing Protocol

The more relevant context parameters are involved in the context-aware routing, the more context changes can be expected over time. For a proactive routing, this either can cause a lot of signalling related to the maintenance of up-to-date routing tables, as each context change would have to be communicated to the members of the network, or some outdatedness of context information would have to be accepted.

For pure reactive routing without any route caching, the frequency of context changes is of minor importance. The routes are determined by route discovery as they are needed, independent of whether the context has changed or not. When there is a frequent need for routes, route caching can be used to reduce the frequency of route discoveries, and therefore the amount of signalling. If the cache time is too long and the context changes are too frequent, the cached routes can of course be outdated if the context has changed in the meantime. So here, reactive routing is not totally independent of the context change frequency any more.

Reactive routing has another advantage over proactive routing when it comes to context-aware routing: By specifying a parameterised evaluation function in the route requests, it provides greater flexibility. Route discoveries with different context choices, different evaluation functions etc. can be performed simultaneously in a network. To achieve the same flexibility in a proactive routing scheme, all **potentially relevant** context information would constantly have to be kept up to date, which requires not only much signalling but also more local memory, which may be a problem for resource-constrained devices like wireless sensor nodes.

So the answer to the question whether a proactive or a reactive routing is more appropriate for context-aware routing depends on several constraints, of which the frequency of context changes, the interval between the needs for a new route, and the flexibility are the most important ones. In case of slow context changes and frequent needs for routes, a proactive routing is the preferred choice, especially if there are low requirements on the flexibility. In case of fast context changes, a high flexibility demand and/or infrequent need for routes, a reactive scheme should be chosen.

In the logistic domain, the positions of all goods and vehicles are part of the context. This means the context is constantly changing. Additionally, the individual entities within the logistic network have different constraints, e.g. with respect to urgency of delivery. Therefore, there is also a demand for flexibility. Although there is also a frequent need for routes, the constantly changing context and the required flexibility makes a reactive scheme more favourable than a proactive one. In the sensor network domain, the choice is less obvious because it depends, for example, on the sensor node mobility and the sensor data transmission interval. But as soon as a mixed use of regular sensor value transmissions and sudden alerts is expected, the flexibility issue also arises here. These reasons lead to the choice of a reactive routing scheme in this thesis.

However, the route request floods in a network with context-aware routing can be more problematic than in e.g. AODV networks. This is due to the fact that the first incoming route request is not necessarily the best one, and therefore later requests from the same route discovery also have to be forwarded. This flooding issue is discussed in detail in chapter 5.

3.3 Protocol Design

This section describes the protocol framework that results from the specified requirements. First, the general protocol features are described, and then the specialisations for the two application areas (wireless sensor networks and logistic networks) are presented.

3.3.1 Generic Protocol Description

As already mentioned, the use of a reactive routing scheme is chosen because frequent context changes would lead to a large signalling overhead in a proactive scheme,and because reactive routing provides more flexibility. The route detection therefore is supposed to be done using route request and route reply messages.

In Section 3.2.1, it was stated that context information has to be included in the routing messages, i.e. in the route requests and route replies. Therefore, while forwarding route requests, nodes have to add context information into the request, either aggregated or individually for each hop. This makes the request propagation similar to the propagation in source routing schemes such as DSR [JM96]. The context information causes a growth of the route request as it propagates. Based on an evaluation of the available context information, a node in the network can decide whether to forward a route request or not. However, the criteria for this decision have to be specified by the source that initiated the route detection. Eventually, it is possible that no request reaches the destination if the choice of forwarding criteria caused all nodes to discard the route request. In this case, the source experiences a timeout. When this timeout occurs, the source has to modify the forwarding criteria and restart the route detection. After a maximum number of subsequent timeouts, the destination will be considered unreachable.

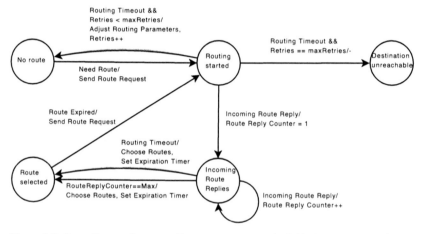

Figure 3.2: State diagram for route discovery process at the initiating entity [WTGG09]

Figure 3.2 shows the states and transitions at the initiator of a context-based reactive route discovery. This state diagram depicts the general behaviour, the complexity is usually higher in specific adaptations to specific application areas.

From the initiator's point of view, the routing is started by sending out a route request message (transition from "No route" to "Routing started") when a route is needed. Simultaneous with sending this message, a routing timer is started. In the "Routing started" state, the entity waits for route replies. If the routing timer expires, the entity's state changes back to "No route", the retry counter is incremented by 1, routing parameters are modified and the routing starts again by transmission of a new route request. If the routing timer expires again and the state is still "Routing started", this procedure is repeated unless the retry counter has reached a maximum value. In this case, the state is changed to "Destination unreachable". If the entity receives its first route reply, the state is changed to

"Incoming Route Replies", which means at least one route option is available. The entity remains in this state until either a maximum number of route replies is received or the routing timer expires. In both cases, a route is selected from those contained in the available route replies (transition to "Route selected"). The selected route remains valid until a route expiry condition is fulfilled. This expiry condition depends on the actual application area where the protocol is used and can be based for example on timers, context changes, etc. In figure 3.2, an expiration timer is selected as expiration criterion. When the route has expired, a new route discovery is initiated.

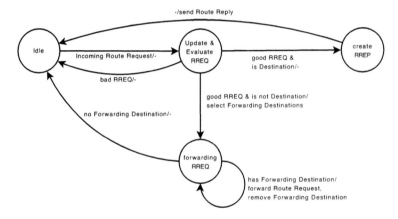

Figure 3.3: State diagram for the route request handling at a node [WTGG09]

Figure 3.3 depicts the route request handling process at a node in the network. When the node is in idle state and receives a route request, it first updates it (i.e. adds locally available information to it) and evaluates whether the route request's metric is acceptable ("good RREQ") or not ("bad RREQ"). If it is not acceptable, the route request is dropped and the node returns to the idle state. If the request metric is acceptable, the node further checks whether it is the destination for the request. If it is, it creates a route reply based on this request and sends the reply to the route discovery originator. Otherwise, it selects its known neighbour nodes as forwarding destinations and forwards the request to them, either by a sequence of unicasts (as depicted), a multicast or a broadcast transmission.

Knowledge base updates   As already stated in section 3.2.1, the nodes that are processing incoming route requests need to have knowledge about how to interpret the context specifications, function parametrisations etc. that are given in the route requests. It was already pointed out that specifying this in detail in each route request would lead to a large message size, and obtaining the information from a dedicated node is also not reasonable. Consequently, each node needs to have its own knowledge base for this, which should still be aligned with the knowledge of the other nodes to assure each node is interpreting the given information in the same way.

When a network is deployed (e.g. in case of a sensor network) or an existing network is enhanced with context-aware decision units (in case of a logistic network), an identical initial knowledge base can be given to all entities. However, it may happen that the knowledge base has to be extended while the network is in operation, as new context criteria or new rules are required. For this case, there has to be a way to update the existing knowledge bases. Generally, there are two ways to achieve this. One way is a push mechanism, the other a pull mechanism.

If an update is relevant for the complete network (e.g. the sensors in a wireless sensor network are supposed to use an additional context parameter), all nodes should receive the update simultaneously, and a flood-based push is the practical way to achieve this. The updates are required to have a unique update ID, so that duplicates can be identified and are not further processed or forwarded. If possible (i.e. the neighbour nodes are known), the updates should be acknowledged on each forwarding hop.

If an entity that starts a route discovery wants to include a context criterion for which it knows (from whatever source) or assumes that it is not present in the current knowledge base, it also does a push by including the required knowledge about the criterion in the current route request. Note that this does not contradict what was said before about including the knowledge in the route request, because 1. this only refers to the route request that is sent when the knowledge is not yet present and 2. only the missing knowledge is included.

In case that a node receives a route request with a context criterion it does not understand, the necessary knowledge has to be pulled. Usually, the node can safely assume that the knowledge is present at the entity from which the request was received. So it can send a request message to that entity, asking for the missing information. The other entity will then retransmit the route request, this time including the required knowledge update.

3.3.2 Specialisation for Wireless Sensor Networks

In wireless sensor networks, context-aware routing can be applied more or less as it is. The routing initiators are sensor nodes that want to send their data, either on a regular basis when their task is a constant monitoring of the covered area, or event driven if they only have to send if something special happens. In both cases, the route discovery itself is identical. The sensor node broadcasts a route request, containing information on which context criteria are relevant and how they should be aggregated. As small messages are desirable in sensor networks due to the sensor nodes' energy constraints, the aggregation of context criteria should be given in a parametrised form instead of specifying a complete formula. As already mentioned in section 3.2.1, this implies the presence of a common knowledge base at the participating nodes. The knowledge that has to be present at the nodes includes the mapping of context IDs to parameters (measurements or status information) that are present at the node. It further includes the generalised functions or rules that are configured with the parameters that are given in the route request, and that are used to evaluate the routes.

As no cluster formation or anything similar is included, the adaptation of this context-aware routing protocol to wireless sensor networks can, according to the classification described in chapter 2.2, be categorised as flat context-aware routing.

3.3.2.1 Reactive Environmental Monitoring Aware Routing

As a sensor network example of the context-aware routing protocol, the *Reactive Environmental Monitoring Aware routing* (Reactive EMA) [WTGG09] was developed for wireless sensor networks as a part of the work done for this thesis. The general idea behind EMA routing is that the environmental conditions influence the route decisions: A sensor network is deployed in a potentially hostile area where sensor node failures occur that are caused by the environment in which the sensors are placed and which they can sense. Examples are sensors that are deployed for fire detection, flood detection or as safety system in chemical plants. Herein, the monitored environmental conditions become part of the context that is relevant for routing. Sensors that are threatened by the sensed phenomena, e.g. fire, chemicals, water etc., have to be avoided as relay nodes in order to prevent route failures.

The EMA idea as such can be used for route decisions in a reactive as well as in a proactive protocol. A Proactive EMA has been presented in [WPTGG08] and has shown good performance. Details about Proactive EMA can also be found in appendix chapter A. In this thesis, however, the focus is on the reactive variant as it implements the reactive framework that is described in the previous sections. In the evaluation presented in chapter 7, simulation results of both the Proactive EMA and the Reactive EMA are shown and compared.

Route Requests in Reactive EMA contain (apart from usual fields such as frame type, source and destination address, sequence number, hop count) a list of hops and a context field. The list of hops simply contains the node addresses on the route, similar to a source routing approach like DSR. The context field is a specialisation of the general context information format shown in figure 3.1 and is depicted in figure 3.4.

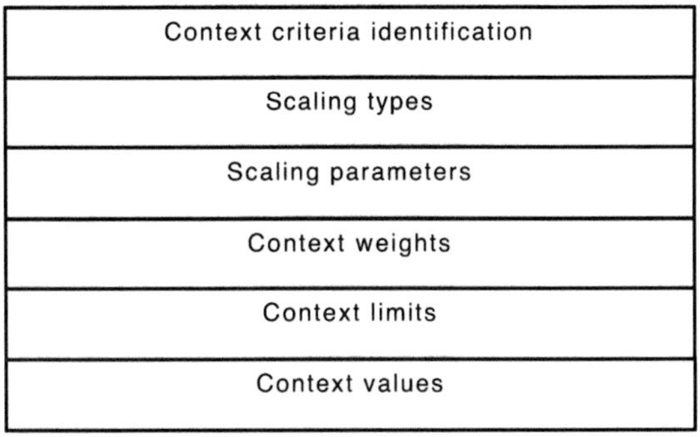

Context criteria identification
Scaling types
Scaling parameters
Context weights
Context limits
Context values

Figure 3.4: Context information structure in a Route Request of Reactive EMA

The "Context criteria identification" contains numeric identifiers for the context criteria being used. This requires that the nodes know how to map the identifiers to context criteria. So each node must have a lookup table that assigns the integer numbers (the identifiers) to context criteria such as signal strength or node health status.

The general way of combining the context criteria is by use of the *Multi-Criteria Context-based Decision function* (MCCD) described in chapter 4, so the general decision function is known in Reactive EMA. Still, there are several degrees of freedom concerning the weighting and scaling, so the general field "Context criteria combination rules" is split into three fields:

1. Scaling types: Numeric identifiers for the scaling function shapes being applied. This assumes the mapping of identifiers to scaling function shapes is known to the nodes. The mappings are most likely to be integrated into the nodes before deployment of the network, but it is as well possible to add scaling functions through knowledge base updates afterwards.

2. Scaling parameters: The parameters to apply to the scaling function shape in order to form the actual scaling function. These values are floating point values.

3. Context weights: The weights being applied when combining the scaled context information. The weights can be either integer or floating point values.

The following example explains the relation of scaling type, scaling parameters and context weights: It is assumed that the identifier "1" refers to a linear scaling of the general form $f_{s,i}(c_i) = k_1 c_i + k_2$ and the identifier "2" refers to a negative exponential scaling of the general form $f_{s,i}(c_i) = k_3 e^{-k_4 c_i} + k_5$ with $k_1, ..., k_5$ being constant parameters. Further, it is assumed that the decision function uses two context criteria c_1 and c_2 and has the form

$$U = (3c_1 + 0.5)^{0.9}(2e^{-0.4c_2} - 1)^{1.5}. \tag{3.2}$$

Then the scaling types field contains the values $[1\ 2]$, the scaling parameters field contains the values $[3.0\ 0.5\ 2.0\ 0.4\ -1.0]$ and the context weights field contains the values $[0.9\ 1.5]$.

The message handling rules are represented by the field "Context limits", which contains forwarding limits for each individual criterion as well as for the overall route evaluation result. Finally, the last field contains the actual values of all criteria.

The order of values in the different fields must be in accordance to the context and scaling definitions in the first two fields. "Scaling types", "Context weights" and "Context values" contain exactly as many items as "Context criteria identification", while "Context limits" contains one more, which is the overall limit in addition to the individual criteria limits. The number of items in "Scaling parameters" depends on how many parameters are required to describe all the scalings defined in "Scaling types".

In the description of the simulated sensor network scenario in chapter 7, the used context criteria (node health, signal strength, hop count) and their scalings are discussed in more detail.

When a sensor node wants to send data to the sink and it has no valid route, it broadcasts a route request. This route request is forwarded by the nodes that have received it until it either reaches the sink or a context limit is exceeded. Each node updates the context values in the route request before forwarding it. Concerning the context limits for route request forwarding, the Reactive EMA has one more restriction than the generic protocol: It can generally be said for wireless sensor networks that the best route between an intermediate node and the destination does not depend on the chosen route between the source and the intermediate node. This means that although the first incoming route request may not be the best, it can be safely assumed that a route A that has a worse overall metric than a route B at a specific intermediate node will not be better than route B in the end, as both routes will share the same path from the intermediate node to the destination. Therefore, the nodes will discard incoming route requests that have a worse overall metric than previously incoming requests that belong to the same route detection. This is done at intermediate nodes which have to forward route requests, as well as at destination nodes which have to create route replies. For this discarding rule, the sensor nodes memorise the sequence number and overall metric of the most recently forwarded or replied route request. So in addition to the limits specified in the route request, the overall metric of previous incoming route requests with the same sequence number serves as additional limit for forwarding route requests or generating route replies. This reduces unnecessary routing traffic. The calculation of the metrics at each node, however, is a limiting constraint for the complexity of the route evaluation function. Due to the nodes' limited computation power, the evaluation function should not use too many context criteria. In the scenario presented in chapter 7, three criteria are used, which keeps the complexity at a scale which the intermediate nodes can handle.

The sink responds to each incoming route request with a route reply if the context values have not exceeded the limits. These replies travel back to the sensor node as unicast transmissions on the path that the route request has found, that means symmetric link conditions are assumed. As the sensor node does not know in advance how many replies it will receive, it uses a timeout and a maximum reply count. If one of those two is reached, the node decides the route for its data. The route is memorised by the node for a predefined lifetime, afterwards it is considered outdated and is dropped.

The route reply message contains the same fields as the route request, but the contents of the hop list and the context fields are not changed any more. The hop list is used to determine the reverse path back to the sensor node that initiated the route discovery.

As already stated, the Reactive EMA is a source routing approach, which means the route decision is done by the source. This is important especially in scenarios with multiple redundant sinks: A proper route decision in a multi-sink scenario can only done with knowledge about the routes to all available sinks, so it cannot be done by one individual sink but has to be done by the source after having received the route replies. To inform the intermediate nodes about the route that should be used, the hop list for the selected route is put into each data packet. In contrast to the hop list, the context fields are not present in the data packets as they are not needed during data transmission.

This routing scheme allows the use of multiple redundant sinks in the sensor network. In this case, each sink replies to incoming route requests, and the sensor nodes elect routes to the most favourable sinks. However, if there are multiple sinks that are not redundant but serve different purposes, the protocol can be extended to cover this, but that is not within the scope of this work.

3.3.3 Specialisation for Logistic Scenarios

Logistic routing imposes a specific issue to the routing process which is not present in other application domains, e.g. in communication networks. In logistic networks, there are different objects which need to be routed (in the following, only vehicles and goods are taken into account), and their routes depend on each other: Goods have to be routed from an origin to a destination, and they have to be transported by vehicles. Those vehicles, on the other hand, have to obtain a route that allows them to cover transportation needs of several goods simultaneously. The problem with the interdependence of the routes is, among others, that the objectives of a piece of good are not necessarily the same as the vehicle's objectives. While the goods primarily have to be at their destination in time and with minimum costs, the vehicles focus more on efficiency, i.e. an optimised use of cargo capacity and/or cost efficiency. In order to fulfil the objectives, goods need information on vehicle routes and vice versa. Figure 3.5 illustrates this interdependence.

Decentralised routing in logistic scenarios means that the moving entities (vehicles, goods) carry out the routing based on local knowledge. If the goods are considered to be passive components that do not perform decisions themselves, all of the routing is done by the vehicles. They have to obtain knowledge about the available transport demand and then find an optimal (or near-optimal) solution for a route and the corresponding load delivered on this route. One such approach, developed as preparatory work for the context-based routing approach in this thesis, is based on the use of genetic algorithms on the vehicle and has been presented in [WPTG06].

In the approach, three different scenarios were simulated:

- **No pickup, no route change**: Vehicles plan their route, based only on information about the locally available load. Then the vehicles are loaded and fully serve the route without any route changes.
- **Pickup, no route change**: Vehicles plan their route based on locally and remotely available loads. They can collect new loads along the route but do not change the route before they have completely travelled their currently planned route. Information about remotely available load is collected by request/reply signalling similar to route discovery signalling in ad-hoc communication networks.

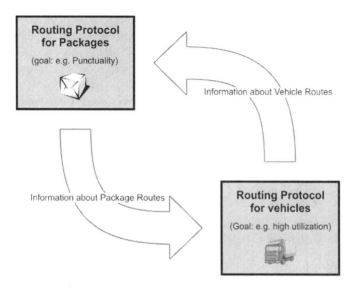

Figure 3.5: Interdependence of vehicle and goods routes [WRTG⁺07], [SRRF06]

- **Pickup, route change**: The major change compared to the previous scenario
  is that the vehicles completely re-evaluate their route and load at each pickup
  or delivery location they visit during their travel. After the re-evaluation,
  parts of the vehicle's current load may have to be unloaded and remain at
  the current location, if the vehicle has decided to continue its route in another
  direction than the originally planned one.

A couple of observations were made during the evaluation of the simulation results. As expected, consideration of remotely available load increases the logistic
efficiency, less vehicles are needed to handle the same transport volume. Frequent
replanning has shown to contain some pitfalls: If the planning is done with long
routes in mind but replanning takes place regularly in early sections of the long
routes, the efficiency can decrease as route changes potentially occur before the
benefits of the long routes become visible. Therefore, if frequent replanning is
done, the early sections of a route have to be prioritised, as those are to be served
before the routes change.

When the goods are intelligent and decision-capable as well, the routing issue becomes more complex. Vehicles and goods determine their routes autonomously, but there is the interdependence shown in figure 3.5 in the way that the vehicles' decisions have an influence on the goods' decisions and vice versa. The result here is that there is not only one context-based routing challenge but two interconnected ones (even more if pallets, containers etc. are also integrated into the process as autonomous actors). The vehicles' routes are part of the context that the goods have to consider for their decisions, and the goods' routes are part of the context for the vehicles. This implies that there has to be a way of exchanging information between the two routing algorithms. These constraints led to the development of the *Distributed Logistic Routing Protocol* (DLRP), which is described in the following.

3.3.3.1 The Distributed Logistic Routing Protocol

The Distributed Logistic Routing Protocol (DLRP), is a route information exchange framework designed for the use by autonomous logistic entities in a logistic network. The DLRP specification was a cooperative work by the author of this thesis and the CRC 637 subproject partners, and was therefore published by the contributing partners in [WRTG⁺07] and [SRRF06]. The preparatory work described above, as well as the decision system used with DLRP and described in chapter 4, and the DLRP implementation in the simulator were conducted by the author of this thesis.

As mentioned before, the challenge in networks with autonomous vehicles, goods etc. is the interdependence of decisions. This leads to the requirement that decisions have to be made public to the other entities in the network. One challenge concerning this requirement is how to provide the information to those entities which need it. This challenge can be illustrated by the following example:

A vehicle has decided to travel a specific route, and this information is of interest to goods along this route. These can be goods that are currently collocated with the vehicle but also goods that are in locations which the vehicle will visit along the route. The most obvious problem here is that the vehicle does not know every entity which is interested in its route information. Broadcasting the information is very inefficient and leads to scalability issues when the network consists of a significant number of entities, so this is not a reasonable option. That leaves the possibility of using indirect communication with the help of commonly known knowledge repositories.

To avoid a single point of failure, which a central knowledge storage would be, a distributed knowledge storage is chosen for DLRP. Assuming that the vehicles transport the goods between locations such as storage facilities, warehouses and distribution centres, in the following subsumed as (network) vertices, these are chosen as places where the information resides. The vertices therefore act as information brokers. When a vehicle or a piece of good (package) chooses a route, this decision is announced to all involved vertices. On these vertices, the route information is available to others.

To realise this, there is an additional pair of messages which extends the reactive routing beyond the pure route discovery mechanisms of route request and route reply messages: route announcements and route disannouncements. The route announcement is a message by which a logistic entity publishes information about its route decision. It is sent to the involved vertices and contains at least information on the chosen route but can also contain additional information such as offered prices, timing constraints etc. The route disannouncement is required for cases when a previously announced route is changed. This is the case for example when the route has been travelled or the logistic entity (vehicle or good) has decided to choose another route.

For the selection of routes, the vehicles and packages need to retrieve information on the current transport demand or available transport capacity and on the current network status. To obtain the information, the concept of route discovery with request and reply mechanisms is used as specified for the generic context-aware routing described in section 3.3.1. Concerning the details, the mechanisms are slightly different for vehicles and packages, so they are explained separately for both.

A package usually has a destination and needs to find a route that leads to this destination. For this route discovery, the package uses the context-aware routing in the package-specific part of DLRP. It sends out a route request containing information about the destination, and about the context criteria relevant for this routing. This route request is sent to the currently associated vertex, which is usually the vertex where it is currently located or which it is approaching if it is currently being transported. The vertex then forwards the request to vertices that are potential next hop locations for the package's route. According to the description for the general protocol in section 3.3.1, each vertex that receives a request adds local context information to it and forwards it again, until the destination is reached. To avoid loops in package routes, vertices that are already present in the route are excluded from the forwarding targets. The locally added context information is based on the known routes of other vehicles and packages, and on the knowledge about the network status itself. The destination then transforms the incoming route requests into route replies that are sent back to the package. The backward path for the route reply can be different from the path that the route request took, as the structure of the communication network used is not necessarily the same as the underlying logistic network. There will usually be several route replies being sent back to the package as there are usually also several route options. As the package does not know in advance how many route replies it will receive, it has to define a timeout how long it waits until it starts the decision process based on the replies that were received so far. Alternatively, it can set a threshold for the number of route replies after which it can start a route decision.

A speciality of the route handling in DLRP-enabled logistic networks is the possibility to have multiple route options for a piece of good. To increase the chance to be transported by a vehicle, a package can select several of the available route options as its route, so that it can join a vehicle that is travelling on any of the selected routes. For example, in the topology shown in figure 6.2, a package which intends to go from Bremen to Berlin may select the alternatives via Hamburg or via Hannover. It will then assign a preference value between 0 and 1 to each of the alternatives, announce all selected alternatives and specify the preference in the announcements. The sum of all preferences for one package must be one, so that the preference represents the probability that the package will travel on that route.

A vehicle's aim is not primarily to reach a specific destination but to transport goods and thus obtain revenue. Therefore, it is interested in efficient utilisation of its transport capacity. The lack of a specific destination distinguishes the vehicle route discovery from the package route discovery: The route requests do not contain any destination information. In contrast, they need to contain a propagation limit, i.e. the propagation has to be stopped and route reply messages have to be sent back to the vehicle when the route request reaches the maximum planning distance which is defined by the vehicle. Everything else is similar to the package route discovery: The vertices add similar information while forwarding the requests, and the vehicle also needs a timer after which it starts deciding based on the received route replies. A difference to the packages' routing is that vehicle routes can contain loops. So vertices may occur in a route more than once. This may lead to a problem that has to be addressed: A vehicle can "get stuck" in an area of the network. For the vehicle itself, this can be beneficial if there is always some available transport demand, but for the rest of the network, it can cause problems because the transport capacity is missing in other areas, so there is a conflict between individual benefits and the overall optimisation in the network. Therefore, to avoid that the vehicle "gets stuck", the route requests are not forwarded along edges that are already being used in the route.

Both the vehicles and the packages have in common that, once they have performed their route decisions, they announce the routes to the vertices that are involved. In case of a vehicle, this is one route, in case of a package, multiple route alternatives can be announced as described before, together with information about preferences whether the route is really taken by the vehicle.

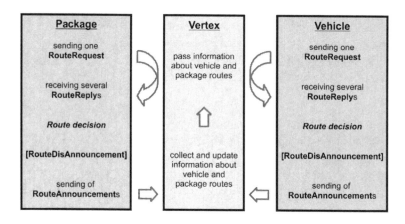

Figure 3.6: Interaction in DLRP [WRTG$^+$07],[SRRF06]

Figure 3.6 illustrates the interaction between vehicles, vertices and packages. The disannouncements that are mentioned in the illustration are used if the vehicle or package already had a route before - which is very likely especially for the vehicles. Before announcing new routes, the old routes are cancelled in this case, which means a disannouncement is sent to all vertices that were involved in the old routes.

Message formats in DLRP   To facilitate the DLRP operation as described above, the route discovery messages described in the general protocol framework description have to be extended.

Similar to the route request messages defined for the sensor network specialisation Reactive EMA, the DLRP route requests also require a sender address, a hop count or time-to-live and a sequence number. As the DLRP-enabled vehicles and goods both do route discoveries, it is necessary to be able to distinguish between messages from vehicles or goods. As vertices cannot automatically deduct from a sender address whether the sender is a vehicle or piece of good (unless the sender addresses are specifically designed to enable this), the route request messages also have to contain a flag that states whether the message is from a vehicle or a goods item. In case of a message from a goods item, there also have to be fields specifying the destination address and the delivery due time.

Furthermore, due to the significantly different time scales between the communication and the logistic transports, not only a list of hops is required, but expected times have to be specified for each hop. There have to be at least two time fields per hop so that it can be determined when the goods are expected to arrive at a given vertex and when they are expected to leave again. It has to be noted that the times can also be implicitly (e.g. as time-dependent costs) included in the context field.

The context field structure can be the same as specified for the Reactive EMA in figure 3.4. Only the contents are different, of course.

The route reply message structure is either the same as for the route request if it is just a copy of the request, or it is cut down to the necessary contents if the vehicle or package remembers the parameters with which it started the route discovery. This can be safely assumed. In this case, the only remaining part of the context field is the context value subfield. The route reply message is not altered on the way back to the vehicle or piece of good. In contrast to the sensor network scenario, it is not necessary for the reply to travel back on the reverse path as the forward path follows the topology of the logistic network while a more direct way through the communication infrastructure can be chosen for the reverse path.

The route announcement messages are sent as unicast messages to all vertices that belong to the selected route. These messages provide the necessary logistic route information to the vertices, which are at least the following:

- a flag identifying whether it comes from a vehicle or a goods item
- the sender address
- an announcement ID that uniquely identifies the announcement
- the expected arrival and leave times for the vertex
- the next hop
- the route preference in case that the announcement is from goods

Depending on the amount of information that the vertices should have about the routes, the information in the announcement can be more detailed. In the simulation used for this thesis, the announcements contain the complete route.

The route disannouncements are sent if a previously announced route is not valid any more. They have to refer directly to a previously announced route. Consequently, they also need to contain the flag, the sender address, the next hop and the announcement ID of the corresponding route announcement.

In appendix chapter D, actual message sizes are presented for the DLRP messages under a set of additional assumptions that make a size estimation possible.

The DLRP itself only provides the framework for the routing, such as the definition of active participants, their roles and the message flows. The route decision itself can be carried out by various kinds of decision functions. Some simple functions have been presented in [WRTG$^+$07] and other publications, a more complex multi-criteria decision is presented in the following chapter of this thesis.

4 Multi-Criteria Decision Systems

In the design and use of routing methods, the signalling is only one part. Another part is the decision-making, i.e. the algorithm(s) used to decide between route alternatives. Most routing algorithms in communication networks only use a single criterion to decide about the route. AODV as one of the examples given in the introduction of Chapter 2 only optimises according to the fastest found route, as only the route on which the destination received the first route request is replied to the source. The fastest found route is the selection criterion in most of the cases. When the routing is context aware, however, multiple context criteria have to be used. This is the case for the routing approach presented in this work. As there are multiple criteria that can influence the decision, these criteria have to be combined into a multi-criteria decision algorithm.

4.1 State of the Art

Routing based on multiple criteria has been shown for some use cases in communication networks. There are some routing algorithms that use more than one criterion to decide about a route. The algorithms can be classified into some that use the criteria sequentially and others that use them in parallel. Some of them are also explicitly labelled "context-aware".

In this state of the art overview on multi-criteria routing, the original notations from the referred publications are used.

4.1.1 Sequential Use of Multiple Criteria

A prominent routing algorithm that uses multiple decision criteria sequentially is the route decision method in Cisco's implementation [Cis00] of the Border Gateway Protocol (BGP).

The BGP standard itself [RLH06] does not give details about how the decisions about the routes are made, it basically only defines the message exchange and the content of the BGP messages. This is why other BGP implementations can be different from Cisco's. In the mentioned implementation, routes are compared with respect to a list of criteria, going through this list from the most important criterion to the least. As soon as there is a difference found with respect to one criterion, a decision is made and the remaining criteria are omitted. This kind of route decision, although it makes use of several criteria, is not really a multi-criterial optimisation as the more important criterion totally dominates the less important, giving relevance to the less important one only if the routes are totally equal with respect to the more important criterion.

4.1.2 Parallel Handling of Multiple Criteria

There have been some approaches recently to handle multiple routing criteria simultaneously in communication networks.

A multi-criteria routing approach for wireless sensor networks was presented in [LBA$^+$05]. The authors present their *Multi-Criteria Routing* (MCR) algorithm based on three criteria, namely *remaining energy per node*, *power consumption model* and *group membership*. Nevertheless, it is not limited to these criteria. The basic structure of the network is assumed to be a one-sink network with a tree structure rooted at the sink node. For the other nodes, the idea of this algorithm is to have ranked lists of neighbour nodes with respect to each criterion at the nodes, i.e. in case of three criteria, each node is maintaining three such lists. The best uplink (parent) node is then selected according to a weighted sum of the rankings in each of the local neighbour lists. The weights can be adapted to the current network status to react to critical values of some criteria. These weight adaptations are done by the root node, which has to track the network status for this.

Another approach that is targeted towards wireless ad-hoc routing in general has been proposed recently [Tho06], [MTT$^+$06]. This approach focuses on the three parameters *energy*, *latency* and *bit error rate* but is not limited to them. In the approach, a *Normalised Weighted Additive Utility Function* (NWAUF) is used to find the best route with respect to the set of criteria. This NWAUF is based on normalised criteria values and weights between 0 and 1 with a cumulative sum of 1. For a set of criteria denoted by $i = 1, 2, \ldots, k$ and a set of route alternatives a_j with $j = 1, 2, \ldots, n$, the NWAUF is defined as:

$$U(a_j) = \sum_{i=1}^{k} w_i f'_{i,j} \text{ for route alternative } j \tag{4.1}$$

where w_i is the weight of criterion i and $f'_{i,j}$ the normalised value of criterion i for alternative a_j, normalised according to

$$f'_{i,j} = \frac{f_{i,j} - f_{i,min}}{f_{i,max} - f_{i,min}} \tag{4.2}$$

with $f_{i,j}$, $f_{i,min}$ and $f_{i,max}$ being the current value, the minimum and the maximum for the respective criterion. The normalisation of values for each criterion is crucial as the criteria usually have different ranges of values, and a criterion which is measured in large numerical values would otherwise dominate other criteria. The normalisation reduces each criterion to a range between 0 (worst) and 1 (best), so all criteria have the same impact to the overall result when they are used with the same weights.

The authors compare the usage of their multi-criteria approach on a global route optimisation to the usage in a distributed optimisation. While the global approach has full knowledge of the network, the distributed approach assumes only that the knowledge about the network is limited, and distance-vector based tables are maintained at each node. Simulation results show that the selected routes in the distributed routing are in most cases the same as the routes that the global multi-criteria routing provides. It is pointed out that the distributed approach, although not having the full network knowledge, performs nearly as good as the one with global knowledge, while it is better feasible in large-scale networks where the high complexity prevents a global optimisation.

The most significant difference between the two multi-criteria routing methods MCR and NWAUF is the point of aggregation within the process of route evaluation. In MCR, there is a separate evaluation and ranking for each of the criteria before the multi-criteria ranking is determined based on the separate rankings. The drawback of this method is that by only using the ranking positions in the aggregation, some information is lost. For example, the difference between two routes with respect to the individual criteria may get lost. This can be illustrated by an example with the following assumptions:

- three equally weighted criteria
- two routes A and B
- A is just marginally better than B for two criteria
- B is much better than A with respect to the third criterion

If only the ranking positions are used in the aggregated evaluation, route A wins because it is better for two criteria and only worse for the third. Common sense would state here that B should instead be the correct choice, as it is better with respect to the only criterion where a *significant* difference is observed.

In contrast to that approach, the NWAUF determines one value for the weighted aggregation of all involved criteria. This means the significance of differences in criterion values is better represented in this solution. The drawback here is that the criteria cannot just be added using their actual values, but the values have to be normalised as described above. To normalise them to values between 0 and

1, however, their possible minimum and maximum values have to be known, that means more a-priori knowledge about the criteria is required. Depending on the criteria to be observed, this can be a more or less critical issue.

4.1.3 Multiple Criteria in a Combined Cluster/Chain Approach

An approach that is combining hierarchical routing with simultaneous use of clusters and chains has been presented in [HH06]. It is labelled as *Cluster and Chain based Energy*Delay Efficient Routing Scheme (C^2E^2S)*. The intention behind this approach is to combine the advantages of both forms of hierarchical routing. In this approach, the network is divided into local multi-hop clusters, based on the optimised cluster formation method for multi-hop clusters defined in [BC03]. In this formation method, an optimal probability p to become a cluster head is calculated based on the sensor density λ and the size of the covered area. Furthermore, the maximum hop distance to a cluster head is denoted as

$$k = \left\lceil \frac{1}{r} \sqrt{\frac{-0.917 \ln(\alpha/7)}{p\lambda}} \right\rceil \tag{4.3}$$

where r is the communication range and α is a parameter related to the probability that all nodes are within at most k hops distance from a cluster head. If α is very small, it is almost certain that all nodes are within that range.

In C^2E^2S, the communication from the cluster heads to the base station (one single base station is assumed) is accomplished via chains. The authors state that it is theoretically possible that the cluster and chain formation may be either done in a distributed fashion by the sensor nodes or centrally by the base station, the results they show are obtained by the latter option.

For the routing within a cluster, the cluster is first partitioned according to the hop distance to the cluster head. Then, the least cost routes from sensors in each partition to the cluster head are obtained. This is where multiple criteria are taken into account. The cost function is a weighted sum of the following criteria:

- The communication cost (transmission energy) between a pair of nodes, proportional to the squared distance between the nodes
- The propagation delay, which is proportional to the distance
- The residual energy of the receiving node
- The number of incoming connections the receiving node has.

This cost sum is then to be minimised for a route from sensor to cluster head in the cluster. For the minimisation, the authors propose a common Dijkstra [Dij59] algorithm.

The chain formation starts at the cluster head that is farthest away from the base station. This cluster head becomes the temporary head of the chain. Then the closest cluster head that is not yet part of a chain becomes the next element of the chain and becomes the next temporary cluster head. This procedure is continued until the base station is closer than the next remaining cluster head. Then the base station is added to the end of the chain and the chain is completed. If there are still cluster heads remaining, the chain formation is started again for the remaining cluster heads.

The authors compare their algorithm to LEACH-C, hierarchical PEGASIS and HEED (see chapter 2 for these) with respect to communication overhead, network lifetime, delay, dissipated energy and energy*delay and show that their algorithm shows a good competitiveness compared to those.

4.1.4 Fuzzy-logic Approach for Multi-criteria Route Decisions

Energy and Mobility-aware Geographical Multipath Routing (EM-GMR) [LR05] is a routing scheme for wireless sensor networks that combines three context attributes: relative distance to a sink, remaining battery capacity and mobility of a node. Concerning the mobility, it has to be noted that it is only used in a scalar form indicating the speed but not the direction of movement.

Each of the three context attributes is mapped to three fuzzy levels (*low, moderate, high* resp. *near, moderate, far*) where triangular membership functions are used for the *moderate* level, and trapezoidal membership functions for the other levels (4.1).

As all fuzzy levels can be combined with each other, this leads to a total of $3^3 = 27$ fuzzy logic rules. The result of these rules is the probability that the corresponding node will be elected as forwarding node for the sender's data. It is expressed as a fuzzy set with 5 levels: Very weak, weak, moderate, strong, very strong.

Each node maintains a neighbour list which is sorted by the 5 fuzzy levels. This neighbour list is kept up-to-date by periodic beacons which are sent out by each node. When data is being sent, the sending node chooses the topmost M nodes from the list as possible forwarding nodes. Then it sends a route notification (RN) to these nodes requesting whether they are available for data forwarding. If the nodes are currently available (i.e. not busy), they send a reply back, indicating that they are free. Then the data is multicasted to all nodes that have indicated to be available, thus establishing a multi-path routing.

The EM-GMR algorithm is evaluated in comparison to a Geographical Multipath Routing (GMR) which only uses the geographic distance as a routing crite-

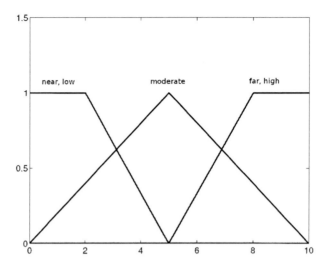

Figure 4.1: Fuzzy levels in EM-GMR [LR05]

rion. The authors show that the GMR is significantly outperformed by the EM-GMR in terms of network lifetime, frame losses and link failures.

4.1.5 Context-aware Routing with Context Prediction

A routing protocol that is explicitly labelled as context-aware is the Sensor Context-Aware Routing protocol (SCAR) [MM06]. It is an adaptation of the Context-Aware Routing protocol (CAR) [MHM05] to wireless sensor networks. SCAR utilises movement and resource predictions for the selection of the data forwarding direction within a sensor network.

In SCAR, each node evaluates the change rate of its connectivity, its collocation with sinks and remaining energy resources. Based on the history of these parameters, a prediction is made using time series forecasting and the forecasted values are combined into a delivery probability for data delivery to a sink. This combination is computed locally on the node by a weighted summation of utility functions related to each of the context criteria. Information about the current delivery probability and the available buffer space is periodically exchanged with the neighbour nodes.

Each node keeps an ordered list of neighbours sorted by the delivery probability. When data is to be sent, it is multicasted to the first R nodes in the list, thus exploiting multiple paths to increase the reliability of delivery. The data sent to the node with the highest delivery probability is labelled as *master copy*, all others as *backup copies*. Backup copies are overwritten if the buffer is full, while a master copy has to remain intact until the data is delivered to the sink.

The algorithm is evaluated by the authors in a follow-up publication [PMM07] against a random message forwarding scheme in a scenario with mobility and intermittent connectivity. According to the simulation results, SCAR shows its advantages mainly in networks where the nodes are sparsely distributed and thus have low connectivity.

4.2 Multi-criterial Optimisation Function for Context-based Routing

The presented state of the art for multi-criteria routing is used as a basis and inspiration for a decision system that can be used in multi-criteria context-based routing.

For multi-criteria context-based routing, an optimisation concept is required that provides the possibility to handle the multiple criteria in a route evaluation function to select the best route. The requirements on the function are the following:

- combination of all criteria into one measure that evaluates the route
- criteria must be weighted according to their importance
- different characteristics of each criterion should be respected, i.e. for some criteria, a non-linear mapping of values to their quality has to be possible
- a single criterion must be able to make a route impossible, e.g. if a sensor node does not have enough remaining energy to participate in a route, it is irrelevant whether all other criteria have "perfect" values.

Looking at the multi-criteria approaches MCR and NWAUF presented in previous subsections, both of them do not fulfil these requirements. Using separate rankings for each criterion and just combining the ranking positions, as in MCR ([LBA+05]), is far from being applicable as a suitable concept here. The NWAUF approach fits better, but it still has some deficiencies. Especially, it does not fulfil the third and fourth requirement of the given list. Still, some ideas of the NWAUF concept are utilised.

To represent different characteristics of each criterion, the normalisation of the criteria values to the interval $[0, 1]$, which is done linearly in NWAUF ([MTT+06]), can be replaced by a characteristic scaling function. This function has to fulfil the following:

- it has to be defined for all possible values of the represented criterion
- its values have to be in the interval $[0, 1]$ for all values of the criterion
- its maximum value has to be 1
- its minimum can be any value in the interval $[0, 1]$.

In contrast to the maximum value, the minimum value can be anything in the interval. A nonzero minimum reduces the impact of a bad value of the represented criterion to the overall evaluation. In Subsection 4.2.1, however, it is pointed out that there have to be additional considerations with respect to fairness among the criteria that impact on the choice of the scaling function.

As scaling function, any shape that fulfils the given restrictions is possible, however, it is useful to specify some basic parameterised scaling functions which can be used for different criteria by application of a different set of parameters. Examples for basic functions that can be thought of are given in the next subsection.

If an additive combination of the criteria in conjunction with a scaling function as described is used, this still does not fulfil the requirement that it should be possible to exclude a route based on a bad value of just one criterion, as a 0 for one criterion does not make the complete result 0. An option to achieve the requirement is to use the logarithm of the scaled criterion, $\ln(f_{s,i}(c_{i,j}))$, in the sum terms (with $f_{s,i}$ being the scaling function and $c_{i,j}$ the value of the criterion C_i for alternative j). Doing this, the resulting evaluation function is a function of the form

$$U_j' = \sum_{i=1}^{k} w_i \ln(f_{s,i}(c_{i,j})) \text{ for alternative } j. \tag{4.4}$$

The given requirements for the route evaluation function are fulfilled by this equation. However, the disadvantage of this function is that the range of U_j' is no longer in the interval $[0, 1]$ but in the interval $[-\infty, 0]$, which makes it more complicated to be handled. Additionally, the interpretation of values is less straightforward if the scale is only limited at one end. As the addition of logarithms of values corresponds to the multiplication of the values, the target function can be changed into a product of the criteria where the weights w_i go into the exponents:

$$U_j = \prod_{i=1}^{k} (f_{s,i}(c_{i,j}))^{w_i} \text{ for alternative } j. \tag{4.5}$$

This function fulfils all four criteria that are given at the beginning of this subsection. Further, its value range is in the interval $[0, 1]$ given that all $f_{s,i}$ are in that interval. This means it is easier to handle than the function given in equation 4.4, and as the lower and upper limits are finite, results can easier be judged whether they are good or bad. Therefore this function is chosen to be the *Multi-Criteria Context-based Decision function* (MCCD) that is used in this thesis.

Some notes on this multiplicative evaluation in MCCD compared with an additive evaluation as in NWAUF:

1. As the neutral element of multiplication is 1, and the neutral element of addition is 0, the aggregation of criteria "behaves" a little different. While in an additive aggregation the good criteria (scaled value = 1) have the most impact to the result, thus making the result good, a criterion with a value of 1 does not change anything in a multiplication. In the multiplicative aggregation, bad values are making the result bad, and a value of 0, which has no effect on the sum in the additive aggregation, has the maximum impact in the multiplicative aggregation by turning the product into 0. So in short:

   - Additive aggregation: Poor values have no influence, good ones improve evaluation result
   - Multiplicative aggregation: Poor values degrade the evaluation result, good values do not change it

2. While in additive aggregation, the weights w_i have to be in the interval $[0, 1]$ and the sum of the weights as well, the weights used in a multiplicative aggregation are only restricted to the interval $[0, \infty]$. In both forms of aggregation, a weight of 0 means the criterion has no effect on the evaluation. In practical applications, however, one has to be aware that high weights in the exponent have the potential to impose a problem as they can quickly turn a value between 0 and 1 into 0 (or at least below the numeric resolution of the computation device that evaluates it).

4.2.1 General Characteristic Scaling Functions

The scaling functions mentioned in the section before are utilised to project the value range of a context criterion to an interval between 0 and 1. The function being applied to a criterion has to be an individual function for this specific criterion. Generally, all functions where $f(x) \in [0, 1] \forall x$ are possible scaling functions. Dependent on the characteristics of the context criterion and the requirements (possible value range, target value range etc.), different characteristic scaling functions have to be applied. These can be both continuous or defined in sections.

Criterion target characteristic	criterion value range	possible scaling functions
Monotonically decreasing	$[0, \infty]$	$f_s(x) = e^{-kx}$ $f_s(x) = \frac{1}{kx+1}$
Monotonically increasing	$[0, \infty]$	$f_s(x) = 1 - e^{-kx}$ $f_s(x) = 1 - \frac{1}{kx+1}$
Linear	$[x_{min}, x_{max}]$	$f_s(x) = ax + b$
Step	$[-\infty, \infty]$	$f_s(x) = \begin{cases} 1 & \text{if } x > x_0 \\ 0 & \text{otherwise} \end{cases}$
"Smooth" step upwards	$[-\infty, \infty]$	$f_s(x) = \frac{1}{2}\left(1 + \text{erf}\left(\frac{x-\mu}{\sigma\sqrt{2}}\right)\right)$
"Smooth" step downwards	$[-\infty, \infty]$	$f_s(x) = \frac{1}{2}\,\text{erfc}\left(\frac{x-\mu}{\sigma\sqrt{2}}\right)$
Bell curve	$[-\infty, \infty]$	$f_s(x) = e^{-kx^2}$

Table 4.1: General characteristic scaling functions

The choice of scaling functions is crucial for the proper functioning of the evaluation: Even when all scaling functions are mapping their corresponding criterion to the same value range, it is still possible that one criterion dominates the evaluation depending on the distribution of its scaled values within the value range, compared to that of the other parameters. Therefore, a "fairness" has to be achieved among the scaled context parameters used in the evaluation. Fairness in this case does not mean that all scaled parameters should have the same distribution within the $[0, 1]$ interval but that the influence of a criterion on the evaluation is really representing its importance. This also implies that a compensation among the parameters is possible if they are equally important (e.g. data rate vs. costs per time: equally weighted, a doubled data rate is supposed to compensate double costs per time). This means if the overall evaluation should "behave" the same for two or more criteria, those criteria must use the same characteristic scaling function. If the behaviour should be inverse for two criteria, inverse scaling functions are to be chosen.

In practice, as the idea is to use parameterised scaling functions that only require transmission of the parameters in the route requests, a set of standard scaling functions is required which can then be parameterised.

Table 4.1 lists some general scaling functions. These can, of course, be modified by shifting or multiplication as long as the results remain in the range $[0, 1]$.

Criterion	Symbol	Scaling function requirements
Energy consumption	E_{route}	monotonically decreasing, $f_1(0) = 1, f_1(\infty) = 0$
Delay	d_{route}	monotonically decreasing, $f_2(0) = 1, f_2(\infty) = 0$
Group membership (aggregability)	G	discrete, $f_3(G) = 1$ if aggregable

Table 4.2: Routing criteria for example scenario

However, shiftings and multiplications have to be carefully dimensioned as they potentially compromise the aforementioned fairness between the criteria.

The functions specified for a smooth step upwards and downwards are the cumulative distribution function (cdf) and the complementary cumulative distribution function for a normal distribution. Of course, other functions with similar characteristics could also be used there.

For context parameters with more complex characteristics, a function which is defined in sections can be used where for each section, a separate scaling function is applied. For example, a scaling function can consist of a section with a linear scaling and another section with a negative exponential scaling characteristic. Examples for section-wise defined functions are given later in this thesis when actual representations for logistic and for sensor networks are introduced.

4.2.2 Example for a Multi-criteria Evaluation Function

In the following, an example for the use of the MCCD is given. This example is a sensor network scenario. The criteria that are used in the scenario are energy consumption, delay and group membership (see Table 4.2). Group membership here means that the sensors have something in common so that their data can be aggregated. This example, however, is not the sensor network setup being used in the evaluation later on, but a simplified one for explanation of how the multi-criteria decision function is used. For the actual setup used in the evaluation, please refer to section 7.2.

Energy consumption and delay are both criteria that can have values between 0 and ∞, and low values are desirable. This means the scaling function has to be monotonically decreasing for increasing values. The scaling functions for energy consumption and delay can be represented by negative exponential functions, as these functions fulfil the constraints:

$$f_1(E_{route}) = e^{-a*E_{route}} \tag{4.6}$$
$$f_2(d_{route}) = e^{-b*d_{route}} \tag{4.7}$$

Here, a and b are parameters that are specific to the steepness of the decrease and are specifically chosen dependent on the actual value range that the criteria cover.

The group membership criterion has to be represented in another function. This function should have the value 1 if the next node is member of the same group G_0 as the sending node, and a lower value otherwise. As missing aggregability usually will not make the usage of a route impossible, the function should not be 0 for any group membership. This leads to a function of the kind

$$f_3(G) = \begin{cases} 1 & \text{if } G = G_0 \\ f_{3,min} & \text{otherwise} \end{cases} \tag{4.8}$$

where $f_{3,min}$ is a value in the interval $]0, 1[$.
With criteria weights w_1, w_2 and w_3, 4.5 leads to

$$U = \begin{cases} (e^{-a*E_{route}})^{w_1} (e^{-b*d_{route}})^{w_2} & \text{if } G = G_0 \\ (e^{-a*E_{route}})^{w_1} (e^{-b*d_{route}})^{w_2} f_{3,min}^{w_3} & \text{otherwise} \end{cases} \tag{4.9}$$

or, more simplified:

$$U = \begin{cases} e^{-(w_1 a*E_{route}+w_2 b*d_{route})} & \text{if } G = G_0 \\ e^{-(w_1 a*E_{route}+w_2 b*d_{route})} f_{3,min}^{w_3} & \text{otherwise} \end{cases} \tag{4.10}$$

This result is then used to choose the most appropriate route.

5 Analytical Examination of Route Discovery Traffic

The task of finding an optimal path with respect to multiple criteria, as it is intended in the proposed context-based routing, can be categorised in the category of so-called *Multi-Constrained Path* (MCP) problems.

It was shown in 1984 that problems of this category are generally NP-complete in case of two or more constraints [Jaf84]. Therefore, the solution space for such a problem grows dramatically with the size of the considered scenario. An exhaustive search in the solution space soon becomes impossible.

Actually, routing algorithms that detect routes by flooding route requests into the network and evaluation of the returned route replies do not require an explicit search in the solution space, but the detection using the forwarding of route requests can be seen as an implicit search. As without any limitations, all possible routes are found during the detection, there are as many route replies as there are solutions in the solution space, and a lot more route requests as it takes multiple route requests to find a route. Here, the growth of the solution space leads to an immense increase in control traffic. This leads to high costs and congestion in communication networks.

Consequently, it is desirable to find a possibility to reduce the complexity of the problem and thereby the induced routing traffic by shaping or reducing the solution space.

This chapter covers the analysis of routing traffic that is generated during route discovery. For small scenarios with known topologies, the number of paths and the amount of messaging can be determined exactly with the help of trees that represent all possible paths. When the network size is large, however, the amount of possible source-destination pairs also increases and thereby also the number of trees. The size of the trees grows as well, of course. Therefore it is more useful to develop reasonable estimates of the traffic instead of counting all branches of all trees.

5.1 Solution Space Description

For the analysis of the solution space, two different kinds of routing have to be considered: destination-oriented routing and destinationless routing. Destination-oriented routing is the "normal" routing that usually happens in communication networks, and it also applies for goods in logistic networks. In this type of routing, a route towards a destination is sought.

Destinationless routing may seem a strange concept, because it implies that a route is being sought without any specific destination. This fits everywhere where the main objective is to use resources efficiently, independent of individual destinations. In logistic networks, this applies to the routing of vehicles.

5.1.1 Destination-oriented Routing

The solution space is spanned by all possible solutions to the evaluation function. For destination-oriented routing, this refers to the possible paths between a pair of nodes. In a fully connected mesh of N nodes, there are loop-free paths with lengths ranging from 1 (direct connection) to $N-1$ (all nodes are involved). There is exactly one path with a length of 1, for a length of 2, there are $N-2$ paths (there is exactly one path for each possible intermediate node), for a length of 3, there are $(N-2)(N-3)$ paths (one for each possible pair of intermediate nodes) and so on. The general term for the number of paths with a length of i is $(N-2)(N-3)\cdots(N-i) = \frac{(N-2)!}{(N-i-1)!}$.

Summing up the paths for all possible path lengths from 1 to $N-1$, the number of possible loop-free paths between two nodes is

$$n_{paths,full} = \sum_{i=1}^{N-1} \frac{(N-2)!}{(N-i-1)!} = \sum_{i=1}^{N-1} \frac{(N-2)!}{(i-1)!}. \tag{5.1}$$

The last part of this equation can easily be understood if the row of summands are written down: it is simply the same row backwards. This equation gives the upper bound of the number of valid solutions for loop-free paths in a network. Due to the factorial term, the solution space grows immensely with growing network size. For example, a fully connected mesh of 10 nodes has already 109601 possible loop-free paths between any pair of nodes. Assuming a route discovery process where route request messages are sent over the network and use (discover) all of the loop-free paths, route requests are propagating on each link of each path. But due to the branching at each node, the number of route requests fortunately is not the sum of all path lengths, as multiple paths share common subpaths. In fact, a path with a length of $i > 2$ shares all but 2 links with a path of a length of $i - 1$ *in a full mesh.* Paths with a length of $i \leq 2$ do not have shorter paths with which they share links. This can be seen from figure 5.1 which shows the tree of all loop-free paths from node 1 to node 2 in a 5-node full mesh.

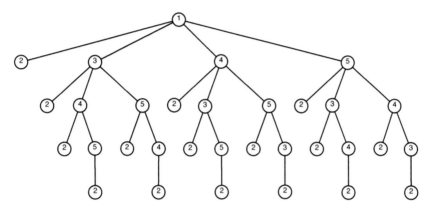

Figure 5.1: Tree of paths between nodes 1 and 2 in a 5-node mesh

Considering this, the total amount of route request transmissions accumulates to

$$n_{RREQs,full} = \sum_{i=1}^{N-1} \left[\min(i,2) \frac{(N-2)!}{(N-i-1)!} \right].$$ (5.2)

As the number of route replies equals the number of loop-free paths, the total amount of route discovery messages is

$$n_{RREQs+RREPs,full} = \sum_{i=1}^{N-1} \left[(\min(i,2)+1) \frac{(N-2)!}{(N-i-1)!} \right].$$ (5.3)

In the 10 node example, these are as much as 219201 route request messages being transmitted during one route discovery, and together with the route replies, the total amount of route discovery messages is 328802. This clearly shows how much traffic can be generated in a route discovery.

However, a network is usually just a partial mesh, i.e. even though the complete network is still connected, the number of direct node-to-node connections is less. This makes the solution space smaller but also more complicated to describe exactly, as the restrictions have to be represented in the solution space description.

In a network with N nodes where each of the nodes has on average K edges (the nodes have average degree of K), more detailed knowledge about the topology of the network is required in order to specify the exact number of loop-free paths. In the general case, i.e. without this more detailed knowledge, only estimates can be made for an upper bound or an average number of paths between a pair of nodes. In this case, a path existence probability P_{path} that depends on N, K and the path length l is introduced into the formula for the amount of paths:

$$n_{paths,partial} = \sum_{i=1}^{N-1} \left[\frac{(N-2)!}{(N-i-1)!} P_{path}(N,K,i) \right]. \tag{5.4}$$

The probability of the existence of a connection between two nodes has to be taken into account for each partial link in a path. If, as assumed here, only N and K are known, the existence probability of a specific link equals the quotient of the degree K and the maximum number of possible links attached to a node, $N-1$:

$$P_{link} = \frac{K}{N-1}. \tag{5.5}$$

As all links of a path have to exist, the probability for the existence of a specific path of length l is $P_{path} = P_{link}^l$, given that there is no correlation between the existence of the partial links. Taking this into account, an estimate for the number of loop-free paths between two nodes can be expressed as

$$n_{paths,partial} = \sum_{i=1}^{N-1} \left[\frac{(N-2)!}{(N-i-1)!} \left(\frac{K}{N-1} \right)^i \right]. \tag{5.6}$$

As for the existence of a specific path, no correlation between the existence of partial links was assumed, equation 5.6 is not exact. The correlation is related to the topology of the network and will modify this equation further. Without knowledge of the topology, however, the correlation cannot be specified, thus the given equation has to be used as an approximation for the number of paths.

Assuming a network with 10 nodes and an average degree $K = 5$, (5.6) yields an estimated number of 1229.56 loop-free paths between two nodes, which is approximately two orders of magnitude less than in the fully connected network. Having another look at the number of route requests in a route discovery that finds all existing paths, the rule that only two links in a path of length $i > 2$ are not included in a path of length $i - 1$ does not hold any more. Instead, there has to be another estimate on how many links are not included in shorter paths.

If a path of length l exists, then all sublinks obviously also exist. Therefore, the question whether a subpath of length m is already part of a shorter existing path is only dependent on whether there is a subpath which is shorter than $l - m$, and which connects the subpath of length m to the destination.

For $m = l - 2$, there is only one possibility, namely the direct link from the m-th node to the destination. Therefore, the probability that this subpath has already been included in a shorter route is P_{link}. For $m = l - 3$, it already becomes more complex as there is not only a one-hop path from the m-th node to the destination but also several possible two-hop paths. Their maximum amount is $N - m - 2$, as 2 of the N nodes are already source and destination, and another m nodes are already involved in the subpath of length m. The probability that $l - 3$ links of the path were already included in shorter paths is the probability that at least one of those paths from node $l - 3$ to the destination exists, which is 1 minus the probability that none of them exists:

$$P_{inc,l-3} = 1 - (1 - P_{link})(1 - (P_{link})^2)^{N-l-5}. \tag{5.7}$$

Generalising this to any m, the probability that a subpath of length m that belongs to a path of length l was already included in shorter paths is

$$P_{inc,m} = 1 - \prod_{k=1}^{l-m-1} \left(1 - (P_{link})^k\right)^{\frac{(N-m-2)!}{(N-m-k-1)!}}. \tag{5.8}$$

Based on (5.8), and defining $P_{inc,0} = 1$, the number of links (and route requests) $n_{notinc,l}$ not included in shorter paths can be estimated as

$$
\begin{aligned}
n_{notinc,l} &= \sum_{i=2}^{l} \left[i P_{inc,l-i} \prod_{j=1}^{i-1} (1 - P_{inc,l-j})) \right] \\
&= \sum_{i=2}^{l} \left[i \left(1 - \prod_{k=1}^{i-1} \left(1 - (P_{link})^k\right)^{\frac{(N+i-l-2)!}{(N+i-l-k-1)!}} \right) \right. \\
&\quad \left. * \left(\prod_{j=1}^{i-1} \left(\prod_{k=1}^{j-1} \left(1 - (P_{link})^k\right)^{\frac{(N+j-l-2)!}{(N+j-l-k-1)!}} \right) \right) \right]
\end{aligned}
\tag{5.9}
$$
$$\tag{5.10}$$

Inserting this into the estimation for the number of route request transmissions in a route discovery yields

$$n_{RREQs,partial} = \sum_{i=1}^{N-1} \left[n_{notinc,i} \frac{(N-2)!}{(N-i-1)!} \left(\frac{K}{N-1}\right)^i \right] \tag{5.11}$$

and including the route replies, the estimated total number of route discovery messages is

$$n_{RREQs+RREPs,partial} = \sum_{i=1}^{N-1} \left[(n_{notinc,i} + 1) \frac{(N-2)!}{(N-i-1)!} \left(\frac{K}{N-1}\right)^i \right]. \tag{5.12}$$

In the given example, this results in an estimate of 3071.38 route request transmissions or 4300.94 route discovery messages, so this number is also roughly two orders of magnitude lower compared with the full mesh, similar to the relation in the number of paths.

This amount of route request transmissions shows that, without defining limits for the route discovery, the discovery leads to a substantial amount of signalling even in a small-scale network. Existing wireless ad-hoc routing protocols circumvent this by only forwarding the first route request that reaches a node during a route discovery, but if the transmission delay is not the only route selection criterion, this cannot be done because the first arriving request is not necessarily the best one any more. For example, if the link quality is an important criterion, the first incoming route request may come via a low quality route that is fast but error prone. In this case, a later route request that comes via a route with high link quality is more favourable and has to be forwarded as well. This example shows that only forwarding the first incoming route request is not sufficient, but later requests need to be forwarded as well. Therefore, other ways of reducing the signalling are required here, and they have to be based on the route decision criteria that are in use.

5.1.2 Destinationless Routing

In destinationless routing, routes that optimise resource usage have to be found. As there is no destination in this case, another termination condition is needed. A maximum hop count is chosen here as the termination condition. In contrast to destination-oriented routing, routes in destinationless routing are not necessarily loop-free. This means from each node in a route, a hop to all other $N-1$ nodes is possible, regardless whether they are already included in the route or not. The number of possible paths with a length of l_{max}, starting at a specific node, in a full mesh is therefore

$$n_{paths,full} = (N-1)^{l_{max}}. \tag{5.13}$$

From each of the nodes, a route request is sent to all other nodes during a route discovery, so the total number of route requests being sent in this case is

$$n_{RREQs,full} = \sum_{i=1}^{l_{max}} (N-1)^i. \tag{5.14}$$

Using, as before, a network with 10 nodes as an example and setting l_{max} to 5, this leads to 59049 paths (corresponding to the same amount of route replies) and 66429 route requests, so 125478 route discovery messages in total.

In a partial mesh (i.e. a network with less connections between the nodes), the average node degree K comes into account, as already described for the destination-oriented routing. Now, without any knowledge about the exact network topology, only estimates can be made again concerning the number of paths and the number of route requests. If each node has the same degree, the number of possible paths is

$$n_{paths,partial} = K^{l_{max}} \tag{5.15}$$

as each node has K reachable neighbour nodes now. It is assumed again that the paths need not be loop-free. The number of route requests is

$$n_{RREQs,partial} = \sum_{i=1}^{l_{max}} K^i. \tag{5.16}$$

Compared to the fully connected network, it can be seen that the fully connected network is just the special case where $K = N - 1$. In general, the equations show that here, the amount of paths and messages does not depend on the network size any more but only on the node degree and the maximum path length. For a network with $K = 5$ and $l_{max} = 5$, this results in 3125 routes and 3905 route requests, so 7020 route discovery messages.

5.1.3 Validation of the Estimates

To validate the estimates for the number of routes and messages in a network, first two small types of topologies are considered, both regular topologies. One is a 6-node network where each of the nodes has a degree of 3. The other is a 3x3 regular square topology. In these topologies, the number of routes and route requests can be determined by manual creation of trees and counting of the branches in the trees.

The 6-node network with node degree of $K = 3$ is shown in figure 5.2.

Here, the estimated number of valid loop-free routes is

$$n_{paths,partial} = \sum_{i=1}^{5} \left[\frac{4!}{(5-i)!} \left(\frac{3}{5} \right)^i \right] = 9.6086 \tag{5.17}$$

and the number of route requests is estimated as

$$n_{RREQs,partial} = \sum_{i=1}^{5} \left[n_{notinc,i} \frac{4!}{(5-i)!} \left(\frac{3}{5} \right)^i \right] = 20.5379 \tag{5.18}$$

route requests per route discovery.

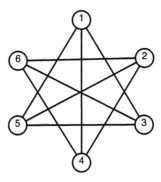

Figure 5.2: 6-node star topology

By direct determination, i.e. counting all options, the average number of routes turns out to be 8.6, being either 8 or 9 for each pair of nodes. The average number of route requests per route discovery is 21.4. So the number of paths is slightly overestimated, while the number of route requests is slightly underestimated.

The 3x3 regular topology is depicted in figure 5.3. It has $N = 9$ nodes and 12 edges (24 if they are considered unidirectional), so the average node degree is $K = 24/9 = 2.\bar{6}$.

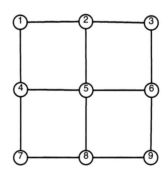

Figure 5.3: 3x3 topology

For this topology, the estimated number of valid loop-free routes is

$$n_{paths,partial} = \sum_{i=1}^{8} \left[\frac{7!}{(8-i)!} \left(\frac{2.\bar{6}}{8} \right)^i \right] = 15.2455 \tag{5.19}$$

and the number of route requests is estimated as

$$n_{RREQs,partial} = \sum_{i=1}^{8} \left[n_{notinc,i} \frac{7!}{(8-i)!} \left(\frac{2.\bar{6}}{8} \right)^i \right] = 41.4541 \qquad (5.20)$$

route requests per route discovery.

Here, it is still possible to determine these amounts directly by creating trees for all possible source-destination pairs, counting the branches on the tree and averaging over all possibilities. Here, the number of paths turns out to be ranging from 7 to 12 with an average of $8.8\bar{3}$ paths per pair. The number of route requests is ranging from 21 to 50 with an average of $35.6\bar{1}$. So the estimate is giving values that are higher than the actual values in this case.

The evaluation shows that while the estimates can give a good hint towards the order of magnitude that is to be expected for the amount of messaging, it is not an exact value. In the 6-node star topology where all nodes are equal, the estimate is closer to the real values.

To validate the estimates for larger scale networks as well, the creation of random networks and the counting of all options in those networks was done on a computer. It should be noted that these are not simulations but exact determinations of the available paths in the generated network instances. The random networks were only required to fulfil two properties: they must not be partitioned, and there must not be more than one direct link between two nodes.

Networks with 10 nodes and a node degree of 5 were already mentioned in an example before, stating that the estimates yield 1229.56 loop-free paths between a pair of nodes, and 3071.38 route requests per route discovery. 10 different random networks with 10 nodes and average node degree 5 were created. In these networks, the average number of paths between two nodes is 781.02 with a sample standard deviation of 114.59, the average number of route requests that would be sent per route discovery is 1947.39 with a sample standard deviation of 269.07. This estimate is again higher than the actual values but can still be seen as a good hint towards the order of magnitude. The difference between the estimate and the values obtained from the generated networks is caused by the following reasons:

- The estimate assumes that there is no correlation among the existence probabilities for individual links. But as the network under consideration has to fulfil certain constraints (e.g. it must not be partitioned), there is actually some correlation. Some links must exist if others do not.
- Some areas of the networks may be sparsely connected, while others are more dense. These inhomogeneous network densities also influence the actual route counts.

A further comparison was done for networks with 15 nodes and an average node degree of 8. Here, the advantage of the estimation formula over the exhaustive path search in the network was clearly visible: while the estimation calculations only took a few seconds on a 3 GHz 64 bit Intel Xeon processor, the search required about 5 hours on the same system.

The estimated number of paths between two nodes in the 15 node network is $1.418 * 10^7$, and the estimated number of route requests is $3.512 * 10^7$. 10 random networks were generated to validate this estimation. In these networks, there are in average $8.477 * 10^6$ paths between two nodes (with a sample standard deviation of $1.0800 * 10^6$), and the average number of route requests that would be sent in a route discovery is $2.0661 * 10^7$ with a sample standard deviation of $2.5039 * 10^7$. Comparisons for larger networks were not done because of the required time for the search, but at least up to the scale for which results are shown here, the estimate can be taken as a good approach to show how much routing traffic could occur in a network where no limitations are applied.

5.2 Solution Space Reduction

As already mentioned, the existing complexity of the multi-constrained routing challenge is a problem for an efficient routing algorithm in a non-trivial scenario. In a distributed routing scenario, especially when route discovery mechanisms are used, this manifests itself in an extremely high amount of signalling per route discovery, a so-called flood. Unlike well-known routing algorithms like AODV, where the only criterion for a route selection is the latency, it is not possible to just discard a route request when another request from the same discovery has already been received before.

Still, the idea of discarding route requests is a promising way to achieve complexity reduction. One method that can still be applied is the limitation of the hop count. Although the route with least hops is not necessarily the best, it can still be assumed that exceeding a certain number of hops will not be beneficial. Another limitation possibility is to use the MCCD with the metrics collected while the route discovery messages are propagating to decide whether to forward the messages. Both methods of flood limitation can also be combined.

5.2.1 Hop Count Limitation

In ad-hoc routing protocols such as AODV or DSR, a hop limit is commonly used to limit the propagation of route discovery messages. This is a feature that can still be utilised in context-based route discovery as long as the hop limit is chosen high enough to find proper routes. The proper choice of the hop limit requires some knowledge about the network topology, because otherwise the limit either does not have much effect on the route discovery traffic (when it is too high) or it prevents route detection (when it is too low).

Destinationless routing already includes a hop limit, as that limit is actually the termination condition for a route discovery, i.e. it decides when a route reply is sent instead of forwarding a route request. Therefore, no specific adaption of the routing traffic estimation has to be made here.

For destination-oriented routing, it is a little different: Here the number of valid routes is reduced to those which are not longer than the hop count limit. In case of a fully connected mesh, the amount of loop-free paths with a maximum length of $l_{max} < N-1$ is now

$$n_{paths,full,l_{max}} = \sum_{i=1}^{l_{max}} \frac{(N-2)!}{(N-i-1)!}. \tag{5.21}$$

For the amount of route requests, it has to be taken into account that there are also route requests propagating on parts of routes that are too long. However, in a full mesh, this only applies to routes that are one hop longer than the limit, and only to the last link of those routes, as the other links are already included in shorter routes. Therefore, the amount of route requests is here

$$n_{RREQs,full,l_{max}} = \sum_{i=1}^{l_{max}} \left[\min(i,2) \frac{(N-2)!}{(N-i-1)!} \right] + \frac{(N-2)!}{(N-l_{max})!}. \tag{5.22}$$

In partially connected networks, the estimated amount of loop-free paths is again similarly modified:

$$n_{paths,partial,l_{max}} = \sum_{i=1}^{l_{max}} \left[\frac{(N-2)!}{(N-i-1)!} \left(\frac{K}{N-1} \right)^i \right]. \tag{5.23}$$

The estimated number of route requests becomes more complex again. Theoretically, parts of routes of any length are relevant, but it has to be determined how many of the links of those routes are relevant. The equation

$$n_{RREQs,partial} = \sum_{i=1}^{N-1} \left[n_{notinc,i}^{*} \frac{(N-2)!}{(N-i-1)!} \left(\frac{K}{N-1} \right)^i \right] \tag{5.24}$$

looks basically the same as without the hop count limitation, but $n^*_{notinc,l}$ is now

$$n^*_{notinc,l} = \begin{cases} \sum_{i=2}^{l}\left[iP_{inc,l-i}\prod_{j=1}^{i-1}(1-P_{inc,l-j})\right] & \text{if } l \le l_{max} \\[2em] \sum_{\substack{i=2+ \\ (l-l_{max})}}^{l}\left[(i-(l-l_{max}))P_{inc,l-i}\prod_{\substack{j=1+ \\ (l-l_{max})}}^{i-1}(1-P_{inc,l-j})\right] & \text{if } l > l_{max}. \end{cases}$$

$$(5.25)$$

5.2.2 Use of the MCCD for the Reduction of Routing Traffic

Using the decision function that is used for route selection for the traffic reduction as well is a reasonable approach to deal with the flooding problem. In [Rea06], this has been done for multi-criteria DSR in ad-hoc networks where the criteria link quality, node energy, hop count and current queue length are used in a combination based on fuzzy logic. Triangular fuzzy membership functions are applied to each of the criteria individually, then the results are combined into two functions: one for a positive caching and forwarding decision and another for a negative decision. Depending on which of the two functions yields the higher result, the request is forwarded or not. As fuzzy metrics are also used to select between route options there, the method of deciding whether to forward is closely related to the method used for route decisions.

In the work presented in this thesis, the multi-criteria decision function is defined differently, so the method for discarding route requests should be adapted to that as well. Based on the solution space that is spanned by the multi-criteria function, a "ruleset" for discarding the requests is expected to achieve a reasonable improvement in the required complexity in terms of signalling. Generally speaking, the forwarding condition defined in the ruleset has to depend on the decision function, the path length and limits defined by the route requesting entity. This leads to an evaluation function for validity of forwarding $V_{FWD}(U,\mathbf{L})$ where U is the decision function and $\mathbf{L} = \begin{bmatrix} U_L & c_{1,L} & c_{2,L} & \cdots & c_{k,L} \end{bmatrix}$ is the set of limits for the decision function and its individual criteria. V_{FWD} is a function with only two discrete values: 0 and 1. It is 1 if all individual criteria and the resulting U are above the limits defined in $\mathbf{L}$: $V_{FWD} = (U > U_L) \wedge (c_1 > c_{1,L}) \wedge \cdots (c_k > c_{k,L})$. In this case, the route request is forwarded, otherwise it is not. A complete path can now only be found if the route request is forwarded on all links within the path. Let $V_{FWD,j}$ be the validity of forwarding on link j. Then the probability for a path of length l to be valid depends on the expected values of the request being forwarded on the individual links. If the limits that are defined are the same along all links in the path, the expected values for the validity of single links are not independent. Assuming further that the evaluation can only become worse from one link to the next, a valid last link always implies that the whole path is valid. Therefore, the validity probability is only dependent on the validity of the last link:

$$P_{valid,l} = E(V_{FWD,l}).$$ (5.26)

For the estimated number of route requests, the validity of a path is not sufficient for a reasonable estimate. Here, a propagation depth D_{Prop} is needed as the route request will propagate until either the path becomes invalid or the destination is reached. This means there are also route requests being forwarded on the first links of invalid paths. Therefore, the expected propagation depth in a path of length l is combined from the validity probabilities of paths with a length less or equal l:

$$E(D_{Prop,l}) = \sum_{i=1}^{l} E(V_{FWD,i}).$$ (5.27)

The propagation depth on a subpath (i.e. a part of a path) depends on the links involved in the path, so for a subpath from link m to l, $m < l$:

$$E(D_{Prop,l,m}) = \sum_{i=m}^{l} E(V_{FWD,i}).$$ (5.28)

5.2.2.1 Destination-oriented Routing

For destination-oriented routing, the above considerations concerning the forwarding limitation result in the following estimate for the number of paths that fulfil the predefined limits:

$$n_{paths,partial,limited} = \sum_{i=1}^{N-1} \left[\frac{(N-2)!}{(N-i-1)!} P_{path}(N,K,i) E(V_{FWD,i}) \right].$$ (5.29)

For the estimated number of route requests, the propagation depth as well as the estimate for the number of links not included in a shorter path are relevant. The estimated number of links of a path of length l that are already included in shorter paths is $l - n_{notinc,l}$. So for that path, only route requests that propagate further than this distance have to be counted. If the propagation depth is lower than this length, the number of requests to be counted is 0, otherwise it is $E(D_{Prop,l}) - (l - n_{notinc,l})$.

So the estimated number of route requests within one route discovery is then

$$n_{RREQs,partial,limited} = \sum_{i=1}^{N-1} \left[\frac{(N-2)!}{(N-i-1)!} P_{path}(N,K,i) \right.$$
$$\left. * \max(0, E(D_{Prop,i}) - (i - n_{notinc,i})) \right]. \quad (5.30)$$

The estimated total number of route discovery messages consequently is

$$n_{RREQs+RREPs,part,ltd} = \sum_{i=1}^{N-1} \left[(\max(0, E(D_{Prop,i}) - (i - n_{notinc,i}))) \right.$$
$$\left. + E(V_{FWD,i}) \frac{(N-2)!}{(N-i-1)!} P_{path}(N,K,i) \right]. \quad (5.31)$$

5.2.2.2 Destinationless Routing

Similar to the destination-oriented routing, destinationless routing messages can also be reduced by the limitation of route request forwarding. The estimated number of paths here reduces to

$$n_{paths,partial,limited} = K^{l_{max}} E(V_{FWD,l_{max}}) \quad (5.32)$$

and the estimated number of route requests is

$$n_{RREQs,partial,limited} = \sum_{i=1}^{l_{max}} \left(K^i \prod_{j=1}^{i} E(V_{FWD,j}) \right). \quad (5.33)$$

5.2.3 Combination of Hop Count Limitation and Limitation According to the MCCD

If sufficient knowledge about the topology is present to apply a hop count limitation, a combination of hop count and MCCD based limitation can be used. Applying this, the discovery process eliminates routes that are too long as well as routes that are too bad with respect to the context. Note that the hop count can also be one of the MCCD criteria, in that case, a limitation based on the MCCD criteria already includes a hop count limitation.

For the estimated number of loop-free paths for destination-oriented routing, only the upper limit of the sum is changed compared to equation 5.29:

$$n_{paths,partial,MCCD+l_{max}} = \sum_{i=1}^{l_{max}} \left[\frac{(N-2)!}{(N-i-1)!} P_{path}(N,K,i) E(V_{FWD,i}) \right]. \quad (5.34)$$

The formula for the estimated number of route requests differs from equation 5.30 only by the replacement of $n_{notinc,i}$ by $n^*_{notinc,i}$, which was defined in equation 5.25:

$$n_{RREQs,partial,MCCD+l_{max}} = \sum_{i=1}^{N-1} \left[\frac{(N-2)!}{(N-i-1)!} P_{path}(N,K,i) \right.$$
$$\left. * \max(0, E(D_{Prop,i}) - (i - n^*_{notinc,i}))) \right]. \quad (5.35)$$

5.2.4 Impact of Different Context Characteristics

As not all context criteria are the same, different criteria characteristics have a different influence on the forwarding limitations. Three different characteristics are analysed here:

- A minimum criterion (e.g. bandwidth)
- An additive context criterion (e.g. delay)
- A multiplicative criterion (e.g. loss probability).

These three characteristics are considered as examples, that means context criteria may also have other characteristics that are not discussed in detail in this analysis.

The minimum criterion A criterion such as the available bandwidth on a route depends on where the bottleneck is. If the criterion focuses only on the minimum bandwidth along a route, only the bandwidth in the bottleneck is relevant, and in other parts of the route, the bandwidth is irrelevant as it is higher than the bottleneck bandwidth. Generally speaking, it is then a criterion where only the minimum is relevant. Given the probability $p_{link,1,L}$ that the minimum criterion c_1 is below its limit $c_{1,L}$ on a link in the network and statistical independence of this probability between different links in the network, the probability that the criterion is below its limit on a route of length l is

$$P_{route,1,L} = 1 - (1 - p_{link,1,L})^l. \quad (5.36)$$

As a consequence, it can generally be said that the route is less likely to be valid if it is longer, because the probability increases that there is a "bad" link in the route. How this contributes to scalability depends on the probability that the criterion on an individual link exceeds the specified limit.

The additive criterion Many criteria, such as delays or other cost measures, cumulate additively along a route. For sums of independent random variables, it is known that the mean is the sum of all individual means. The same holds for the variance.

If the random variables follow a normal distribution, the resulting distribution is also a normal distribution. Assuming that the additive criterion c_2 considered here is distributed according to a normal distribution with mean μ_{c_2} and variance $\sigma_{c_2}^2$, and further assuming that it is a criterion where the limit is an upper limit, the probability to exceed the limit on a link is

$$p_{link,2,L} = \frac{1}{2} \operatorname{erfc}\left(\frac{c_{2,L} - \mu_{c_2}}{\sqrt{2\sigma_{c_2}^2}}\right),$$ (5.37)

and the probability to exceed the limit on a path of length l is

$$p_{route,2,L} = \frac{1}{2} \operatorname{erfc}\left(\frac{c_{2,L} - l\mu_{c_2}}{\sqrt{2l\sigma_{c_2}^2}}\right).$$ (5.38)

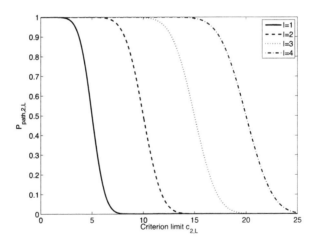

Figure 5.4: Probabilities of exceeding the criterion limit for different path lengths l for an additive criterion with normal distribution

Figure 5.4 shows that the probability of exceeding a certain threshold increases with each hop when the normal distribution has a positive mean ($\mu_{c_2} = 5$ in the figure). This is not surprising as the value of the criterion increases with each hop. This also shows that for a small criterion limit, it is almost impossible that the criterion would remain below the limit on long routes. This is beneficial for scalability: Long routes are generally being cut off if the additive criterion is supposed to remain below a certain threshold, thus avoiding a lot of control traffic that would be created by the discovery of those long routes.

However, if a large value for the context criterion is beneficial, so that an applied threshold would be a lower limit instead of an upper limit, a problem is raised, if the criterion has a positive mean: Long routes would (almost) never be cut off if the first links are acceptable. This also means cutting off a route on the early links may eliminate routes that are good on their later links. Therefore, route request forwarding limits cannot be applied on such routes. The same holds for upper limits on an additive criterion with negative mean.

The multiplicative criterion Criteria with multiplicative characteristics are for example probabilities such as loss or error probabilities, provided they are statistically independent on each link. Considering loss or error probabilities, it is desirable that these probabilities remain below a threshold. Here, it is not sufficient to know the probability that the criterion is below the threshold on an individual link, but the criterion's distribution has to be known to determine the probability that the criterion remains below the threshold for the complete route. Unfortunately, the determination of the product of independent random variables is not trivial in general, as it can be seen from [ST66].

A special case which can be dealt with is when the random variables follow a log-normal distribution. In this case, it is known that the resulting distribution is again a log-normal distribution where the mean and variance of the underlying normal distribution are the sum of the means resp. variances of the individual underlying normal distributions. So if the values for the multiplicative criterion c_3 follow a log-normal distribution such that the probability to exceed the limit $c_{3,L}$ on an individual link is

$$p_{link,3,L} = \frac{1}{2} \operatorname{erfc}\left(\frac{\ln(c_{3,L}) - \mu_{c_3}}{\sqrt{2\sigma_{c_3}^2}}\right), \tag{5.39}$$

the probability to exceed the limit on a path of length l is

$$p_{route,3,L} = \frac{1}{2} \operatorname{erfc}\left(\frac{\ln(c_{3,L}) - l\mu_{c_3}}{\sqrt{2l\sigma_{c_3}^2}}\right). \tag{5.40}$$

Figure 5.5 shows that probability for different path lengths and a log-normal distribution with $\mu = 0$ and $\sigma^2 = 1$. It can be seen that in this constellation, the probability of exceeding the criterion limit increases with increasing route length when the limit is high, while it decreases when the limit is low. There is one point where the probability does not change. The location of this point, however, depends on the μ of the distribution. With increasing μ, it moves towards the point (0,1). Still, it shows the significant difference between multiplicative criteria and additive or minimum criteria: For multiplicative criteria, the probability to exceed a given limit does not necessarily increase with the number of hops in a route.

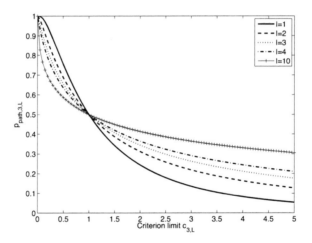

Figure 5.5: Probabilities of exceeding the criterion limit for different path lengths l for a multiplicative criterion with log-normal distribution

As it is usually preferable for scalability of routing traffic that long routes are avoided if possible, a goal should be that the probability to exceed the route request forwarding limit is increasing with increased route lengths. Therefore, it is beneficial for criteria with upper limits such as loss probabilities if a) the point of constant probability is near the (0,1) point and b) the criterion limit is chosen to be on the right side of this point. The larger the criterion value is, the stronger is the bias towards short routes but with decreasing overall probability to drop route requests, which in turn means a higher total number of transmitted requests. For criteria with lower limits (e.g. success probabilities), it is preferable to be in the area left of the point of constant probability.

5.2.4.1 Recommendations for Context Criteria

The previous paragraphs show that with respect to scalability of a reactive context-aware routing algorithm, it is important to have a close look at the context criteria in use. To not get excessive control traffic, there should be at least one criterion which is "benign" in this sense, i.e. which is more likely to exceed a limit on long routes than on short routes. Hop limitation can be seen as the use of such a benign criterion, namely the hop count, which is basically an additive criterion. Anyway, it is definitely better to not only have one criterion that allows route request flood limitation but multiple, as this increases the selectivity of route request forwarding.

The discussions of additive and multiplicative criteria show that it is the chosen combination of criterion characteristics and the forwarding limit that decide whether a criterion can be used for route request forwarding limitation. Still, the choice also has to be reasonable in the sense that it does not prevent good routes from being found.

For additive and multiplicative criteria, the discussion was limited to normal and log-normal distributions respectively. Although these were chosen mainly for mathematical simplicity, the choice can be considered quite reasonable as this kind of distribution is not uncommon, due to the fact that the central limit theorem states that a sufficiently large sum of random variables leads to a normally distributed variable, whereas the product of non-negative random variables converges to a log-normally distributed variable.

5.2.5 Route Rediscoveries

The results for the total number of messages in a route discovery that are shown in the previous subsections would lead to the conclusion that a low forwarding probability and expected propagation depth is always the best option. This is not true as the limitation implies another issue: if the forwarding probability is minimised, the expected values for validity of forwarding on individual links are also minimised, thus minimising the estimated number of valid paths given in equation 5.29. If this number becomes too low, the route discovery is not able to succeed any more if no request reaches the destination. As already stated in subsection 3.3.1, the route discovery is then restarted with less restrictive limits after a timeout expires at the entity that initiated the discovery. This restarted route discovery means a complete new set of route requests, contradicting the intention to reduce the complexity and the network load. Therefore, minimising the expected amount of route requests does not mean minimising the route request forwarding but optimising it so that a route can still be found without having to initiate a second route discovery. Actually, a second route discovery can only be fully avoided if there is no route request limitation, so it would require the full amount of route requests. This is what was to be avoided in the first place.

These considerations lead to the conclusion that there is an optimum between the unlimited forwarding and the need to rediscover a route. This optimum is achieved when the route request caused by required rediscoveries are maximally outnumbered by the route requests saved through forwarding limitation. Assuming that the rediscovery does not use any forwarding limits, the estimated total number of route requests is

$$n_{RREQs} = n_{RREQs,partial,limited} + P_{rediscovery} n_{RREQs,partial} \qquad (5.41)$$

where $P_{rediscovery}$ is the probability that a rediscovery has to be done. This probability depends on several parameters, e.g.:

- the statistical characteristics (value range, probability density function) of the individual context parameters
- the scaling functions used for the parameters
- the weights in the context evaluation function
- the specified forwarding limits
- the network topology.

This shows that the rediscovery probability is quite complex and can probably not be described in a generalised form. A formula for an estimation would have to rely on many assumptions, such as whether

- the spatial distribution of context values is homogeneous,
- there is a correlation between contexts of adjacent links,
- the network topology is regular to some extent, etc.

Therefore, it can be considered impossible to determine a completely generalised expression for the optimum choice of parameters to achieve an efficient route rediscovery.

6 Evaluation in Logistic Networks

6.1 Evaluation Criteria

In chapter 4, decision systems that are used for multi-criteria route optimisation are described. However, they are used for distributed local optimisation within the network, and it cannot generally be assumed that the distributed decisions automatically imply a global optimisation. A performance evaluation of a routing algorithm, however, has to consider the global performance, i.e. the resources that are consumed across the network over time and the overall quality of the discovered routes.

Some of the criteria to be evaluated are protocol-related, others are route-related. The protocol-related criteria describe the effort that has to be spent for the protocol itself, i.e. for the protocol messaging and processing. This means the main criteria here are the route discovery and maintenance message overhead (which can be the amount of routing messages or additional routing data in data messages) and the resource consumption of the routing itself.

Route-related criteria are those that are based on the traffic flows that use the chosen routes. Ideally, the evaluation criteria match the context criteria that are used in the decision function. At least, they have to be related to the decision criteria as otherwise, there is a discrepancy between the optimisation targets and the performance measures used for evaluation.

Generally, the route-related criteria represent the global efficiency and reliability of the applied routing. What criteria are selected exactly depends on the application domain where the routing is applied. Examples are resource utilisation, throughput or end-to-end delay.

In contrast to the route decision function presented in chapter 4, the criteria are not necessarily merged into one single measure, but they are treated separately. In this way, it is easier to identify the criteria where an algorithm has strengths or weaknesses. Through this it is also possible to define trade-offs.

6.1.1 Evaluation Criteria for Logistic Networks

In logistic networks, there are two general categories of measures: Logistic measures and communication traffic measures. The logistic measures contain all measures related to the transport of the goods. The communication traffic is the amount of communication generated by the routing.

6.1.1.1 Logistic Measures

If logistic processes are considered, the main evaluation criteria are, of course, logistic performance criteria. The criteria considered here are introduced in the following paragraphs, and as they closely match the context criteria for route decisions, they are discussed in more detail when the context criteria are introduced.

In logistics, the main criterion usually is economic efficiency. Most measures can be mapped directly or indirectly into monetary costs. Consequently, the costs for the goods and the revenue the vehicles can obtain are evaluation criteria in logistic networks.

Furthermore, it is important for logistics service providers that the goods reach their destinations in time, otherwise they lose reputation in the eyes of their customers. This loss of reputation cannot be expressed directly in monetary value, so the timeliness is to be considered as a separate evaluation criterion. The same holds for the risk of damage: If goods are damaged during transport, the logistic service providers lose reputation as well, so this risk also has to be regarded as an evaluation criterion.

Another measure that will become more and more important in the future is the ecological impact. When talking about ecological issues and logistics, the main issues that come to one's mind are the emissions that are caused by the vehicles. The ecological impact is a parameter that is neither directly related to monetary costs nor reputation, but as regulations for climate protection become increasingly common, such regulations can also be expected to be established for logistic service providers in the future. Therefore, the overall carbon dioxide emissions are a criterion for evaluation.

6.1.1.2 Communication Traffic

The distributed routing itself creates a significant amount of communication traffic, especially for route discovery. This traffic may impose limits for the scalability, as already mentioned in the solution space discussion in the previous chapter. So the volume of this communication traffic is a non-logistic measure in the logistic scenarios.

6.2 Decision System for Logistic Networks

For the use in logistic networks, the MCCD developed in section 4.2 is applied in conjunction with the Distributed Logistic Routing Protocol (DLRP) introduced in subsection 3.3.3.1. This combination implements the context-aware routing concept in logistic networks, with specific decision criteria for vehicles and packages [WRTGG09]. As already described in the DLRP introduction, vehicles and packages are both assumed to be autonomous and capable of decision-making. Therefore, different MCCD functions have to be used for vehicle routing and package routing due to the different objectives of vehicles and packages. The criteria used here are mostly the same as the logistic measures introduced in section 6.1.1.1.

6.2.1 Vehicle Routing

The vehicle route decisions depend on a set of measurable or computable parameters that are not necessarily used directly as context criteria, but context criteria are derived from them. The measures are:

- Transport demand
- Route length
- Travel time required for a route
- Specific route costs (toll etc.)
- Reliability of timings
- Accurateness of transport demand information.

These parameters can be converted into context criteria that are used for route evaluation. There are criteria that specify expected benefits and impacts of a vehicle route, in this case:

- Monetary revenue
- Ecological impact.

Associated to those, there are risks that the expectations are not achieved, i.e. the route leads to less revenue or the ecological impact is worse. These risks state how reliable the current expectations are. These risks are context criteria as well:

- Risk of revenue loss
- Risk of emission goal underachievement.

These criteria and their scaling functions are discussed in more detail in the following pages.

Monetary revenue The monetary revenue contains everything that can directly be mapped to monetary values. This is on the one hand the revenue that is generated by the goods (packages) to be transported, and on the other hand the costs that occur when the vehicle uses a specific route for its transport. In detail:

Revenue generated by packages When a package has selected a route and announces it to the involved vertices, it can include information about its offered price in the announcement, depending on its budget and the chosen route. The vertices thereby have knowledge about the revenue that can be obtained by transporting the package. As the vehicle cannot load more than its capacity, the vertex has to consider this constraint while computing the expected revenue.

Time-unrelated route costs The cost components that are unrelated to time mainly consist of two components: The general costs per km that the vehicle has (fuel, wear etc.) and costs that are specific to a route (especially route toll, ferry costs etc.). The route-specific costs are usually known at a vertex, as these are fixed costs in most cases. The vehicle costs per km are vehicle-specific, so the vehicle has to provide them in the route request.

Time-related route costs Time-related route costs are mainly coupled with the packages' delivery time. If a package gets delivered outside its target delivery time window, a fine has to be paid. As this is package-specific, the package has to provide information on the time constraints and the fines. This information has to be provided individually for each link in the route, i.e. the package has to provide information on a time window when it has to reach the next hop, and a fine that has to be paid if it doesn't reach the location in time. This makes sure that it is not just the vehicle on the last hop that "gets blamed" for a delay, but all vehicles that do not fulfil intermediate targets are responsible. As the delivery fines are associated with individual packages, they depend on the set of packages that are considered to be loaded. The same holds for the previously introduced revenue generated by the packages. Therefore, the two parameters are not independent and their optimisation requires finding the maximum of the difference between package revenue and fines.

Scaling the monetary revenue Obviously, the monetary revenue can have positive as well as negative values. If the revenue is negative, however, serving the route clearly has no benefit for the vehicle. Consequently, the scaling for a negative revenue has to be 0 when the vehicle evaluates the routes. For positive values, the scaled value has to approach 1 for increasing revenue.

Actually, the monetary revenue related to time or travel distance is much more interesting than the absolute revenue for a route, otherwise the evaluation is biased in favour of long routes which have a better absolute revenue but still can have a lower revenue in relation to distance or time. Therefore, the revenue is divided by the travel distance before evaluation.

Concerning the revenue evaluation at intermediate steps for the route request forwarding decision, another aspect has to be considered which leads to different requirements on the scaling: As the monetary revenue is a parameter that can improve on subsequent hops of the route, the scaled revenue has to be greater than 0 as long as the route requests are forwarded. Otherwise, a beneficial route is not found if it has no positive revenue on the first hop but much on the following ones. For the same reason, the forwarding limit should also be chosen such that it does not create this problem. This actually means there should be a very low forwarding limit related to the monetary revenue. The overall forwarding limit (the limit for the output of the MCCD) also has to be chosen in a way so that it only cancels the forwarding if it cannot be expected that the intermediate result can still be improved enough to achieve a valuable route.

During the route request forwarding, there is no knowledge about what the maximum revenue is. Therefore, the scaling function has to be chosen as a function that asymptotically approaches 1 for increasing revenue. When the vehicle is evaluating the received route replies, however, it can retrieve the maximum revenue value from the received replies. This means the vehicle can dimension its revenue scaling with respect to the achievable maximum. This has the advantage that a non-asymptotic scale can be used here, which circumvents the problem that asymptotic scales give only marginally different results for high values, even if the values themselves are significantly different.

Ecological impact   The ecological impact that a vehicle's route causes is a measure for how efficient the transport is in terms of ecological damage that is caused by it. This is a criterion that cannot directly be mapped to monetary costs, so it has to be treated separately. An absolute value for the ecological impact cannot be given easily when trying to consider all ecological consequences. Still, there are ecological criteria that are quantifiable. A good example is the carbon dioxide emissions. If the vehicle's emissions per kilometre are known, they can be calculated per tonne-kilometre (tkm). Sparsely loaded vehicles then have a high output per tkm, full vehicles a lower one. Governments are becoming more and more aware of the need for efficient climate protection, which led to the Kyoto protocol

[Nat98] and follow-up national and international commitments. One of the main foci in this area is the reduction of carbon dioxide emissions. With the European Union already having defined a carbon dioxide emission goal of in average 120 g/km for car manufacturers' model range, it is very probable that there will be regulations to limit the carbon dioxide emissions per tkm for freight carriers' fleets in the near future.

If there is a regulatory limit for the carbon dioxide emissions, the vehicle needs to try to remain below this limit. The scaling function being used here has to represent this. However, as a regulatory limit will probably not refer to single transports but to average values for a complete fleet and a given time frame, the limit is not a hard limit for a single transport operation. A scaling function with the characteristics of the complementary cumulative distribution (ccdf) of a normal distribution seems suitable here. This ccdf is

$$F_c(x) = \frac{1}{2} \, \text{erfc} \left(\frac{x - \mu}{\sigma\sqrt{2}} \right). \tag{6.1}$$

Figure 6.1 shows the application of such a scale to the carbon dioxide balance. The choice of μ is related to the emissions limit that should be achieved, and the choice of σ represents the steepness of the scale.

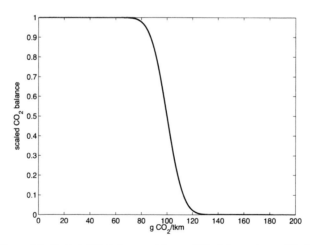

Figure 6.1: Scaled CO_2 balance with $\mu = 100g/tkm$ and $\sigma = 10g/tkm$

In order to react on an exceeded limit during previous transports, the choice of μ can be adaptive: In this case, it has to be reduced if the limit was exceeded in average, and can be relaxed if there was no problem in keeping the limit.

Risk of revenue loss As the transport scenarios are dynamic and there are several (concurrent) actors, a vehicle cannot be sure that the revenue it has calculated for a route is actually the revenue it can obtain in the end. It can happen that the real revenue is less than the expected. This can have the following reasons:

- packages can be picked up by other vehicles before the vehicle reaches their location
- packages being transported to a location by another vehicle may be delayed, thus they are not present when they should be picked up
- variations in the travel time can cause additional delays that lead to fines for late deliveries
- if packages have announced multiple alternative routes, some information becomes invalid when one route is chosen and other routes become obsolete.

Generally, it can be said that information is less reliable the further away (in space and time) their influence on the route is. To explain this, an example is given here: A vehicle is choosing a route where it can load some goods at its current position and some more goods on a position it plans to reach after two hours. Meanwhile, other vehicles are also operating in this area. Regarding the goods at the vehicle's current location, it can be sure that these are available for pickup. On the other hand, the availability cannot be assured regarding the goods at the future location, as other vehicles can come there earlier and pick them up. If those other vehicles have already announced a route there, those announcements are already part of the revenue calculation, but there is a chance that the corresponding vehicle routes are not announced yet.

This reliability actually is not easy to grasp. If historic data is available, either at the vertex or the vehicle, concerning the goodness of forecasts, it can be estimated according to that historic data. If not, the vehicle can only make a guess based on a predefined estimate of the forecast quality. This holds both for the available goods at distant locations and for travel times.

Regardless of whether it is based on historic data or not, the risk of revenue loss specifies a probability that the revenue is below the expected revenue. If there is a cdf that describes the distribution of revenue for a route, the probability to fail achieving a specific revenue can be determined with the help of this cdf. When historic data is used, the vertices have to maintain statistics on the revenues that vehicles have obtained for a next hop. This statistics should not include expected revenues calculated for the future by distant vehicles but only revenues that were really available when a *locally present* vehicle was planning a new route.

This risk then has to be scaled: If there is practically no risk, the scaling should result in a value of 1. If the risk is close to 1, i.e. it is probable that the revenue will not be achieved, the result still has to be greater than 0, otherwise a route with high expected revenue will be impossible just because there is a high risk that this revenue is not reached. Therefore, a scaling function that is monotonically decreasing from 1 to a nonzero value in $[0, 1]$ is required.

The risk as such does not state how large the probable deviation from the expected revenue is. To additionally have some information on the deviation, the risk formulation has to be adapted to allow a tolerance. This means to determine the probability that at least a certain percentage of the revenue will be achieved.

Risk of emission goal underachievement   When the vehicle is planning its route, it calculates an expected utilisation for trips on future links. Dependent on the expected utilisation and the length of the links, an expected ecological impact in terms of CO_2 emissions per tonne-kilometre is determined (see the paragraph "Ecological impact"). If then the actually carried load on those links is less than expected, there is an underachievement of the ecological expectation. The reasons are basically the same as for the revenue loss: goods are not where the vehicle expected them to be because they

- were already picked up by someone else,
- are delayed on a link towards the pickup location
- or chose another route in the meantime.

When the vertices already gather statistics about the transports on outgoing links concerning the expected revenue, they can also include statistics on the vehicle utilisation on those links. Those statistics can then be utilised to determine an average utilisation, and thereby an average value for the emissions. Putting the current expected emission into relation, the risk of underachievement can be determined. Concerning the scaling, this risk should be treated similarly to the risk of revenue loss.

6.2.2 Package Routing

For the package route decisions, the following parameters influence the route decision:

- Available transport capacity
- Travel distance
- Travel time
- Transshipments
- Reliability of the route information.

Similar to the vehicle route parameters, they can be combined into the following context criteria that are discussed in the subsequent paragraphs:

- Route costs
- Damage risks
- Delay risks.

Route costs   This criterion includes all costs that occur along a route. These are the price that is paid to the transporting vehicle(s), storage costs and transshipment costs at vertices along the route. The price for the transport is something that the package announces in its route announcement. In this case, the pricing solely depends on what the package defines as a price. Independent of whether it is a fixed price or a price per km, the package does not need to collect this information during the route discovery as it decides by itself what it offers.

The costs for storage and transshipment, however, are defined by the vertices. For the storage, this is dependent on the package volume and the storage duration, and for the transshipment, it depends on the amount of transshipment operations required during the transport.

If the package becomes delayed, there is an additional cost component: the delay fines. If the delay is due to vehicles not fulfilling their time constraints, the delay fines are forwarded to the vehicles, but if the delay is caused by the package not being picked up (which for example depends on the chosen route and the offered price), the package cannot forward the costs, so they are the package's costs after all.

So, the overall costs for a package are, for a given number n of transshipments, a storage duration t_{stor} and a delay $delay$ at the destination:

$$costs = transport\,price + c_1 n + c_2 t_{stor} + c_3 delay \qquad (6.2)$$

with c_1 as costs per transshipment, c_2 as costs per hour of storage and c_3 as delay fine per hour of delay.

The package usually will have a maximum budget, and the total cost for a route needs to remain below the budget in order to achieve an economically sensible transport. Therefore, the scaling for costs (which, in general, can take any value within $[0, \infty]$) has to be 0 for values above the budget, and can be linear decreasing for values between 0 and the budget. Consequently, the scaling function for the budget can be set to

$$f_s(costs) = \begin{cases} 1 - \frac{costs}{budget} & \text{if } 0 \leq costs \leq budget \\ 0 & \text{else} \end{cases} . \tag{6.3}$$

Risk of damage   The risk of damage can be regarded as a parameter that mainly depends on two factors: The travel itself and the transshipment. Each transshipment bears a certain probability that the package becomes damaged. Further, there is a damage probability per km of travel. These risks may be known from historic data or they may be estimated.

Let the probability of damage during one transshipment be $p_{damage,ts}$ and the number of transshipments be n, and further let the probability of damage during one km of transport be $p_{damage,km}$ and the route length be l_{Route} km, then the total damage probability is

$$p_{damage} = 1 - (1 - p_{damage,ts})^n (1 - p_{damage,km})^{l_{Route}} \tag{6.4}$$

According to this formula, the risk of damage is already a criterion with values in $[0, 1]$, but here, low values are preferred. The easiest scaling here would be to just use 1 minus the risk, but this is not acceptable as any risk of damage that is more than marginal must be avoided. Therefore, a more reasonable way of scaling is to define a risk limit beyond which the scaling returns 0, and a decreasing scale between 0 and this limit.

Risk of delay   This criterion is the risk of being delayed at the package's destination. It depends on the availability of transport volume on a route (when and how much volume is available). Furthermore, it depends on how much time is still left to reach the destination on schedule, and on the variation of travel times. Similar to what was stated in the paragraph about the vehicle's risk of revenue loss, the risk of delay is also usually not possible to be defined a priori, as it depends on the logistic network's dynamic behaviour. If the vertices collect a history of data or maintain a history collected by previously transported packages, statistical evaluation of this historic data can be used to generate estimates for the risk. For the risk of delay, the relevant statistics are of course those concerning the package's time spent at vertices and on edges. From historic values, the mean and the variance for these durations can be determined. The mean values then have to be used to achieve a more appropriate estimate for the arrival time at the destination, while under the assumption that the individual time components on a route are each normally distributed and independent, the variances can be added to determine an overall time variance for the route. Under the mentioned assumption, the resulting distribution is also a normal distribution. Now that an estimated mean and variance are known for the arrival time at the destination, the risk of delay is the probability that the arrival time is later than the due time, and it can be determined with the help of the ccdf of the expected arrival time:

$$p_{delay} = \frac{1}{2} \text{ erfc} \left(\frac{t_{Due} - t_{Arr}}{\sigma_{Arr} \sqrt{2}} \right). \tag{6.5}$$

This risk then has to be scaled: If there is practically no risk, the scaling should result in a value of 1. If the risk is 1, i.e. it is certain that the package will be delayed, the result still has to be greater than 0, otherwise a package that is already overdue does not find a route any more and thus will not be transported. Therefore, a scaling function that is monotonically decreasing from 1 to a nonzero value in $[0, 1]$ is required. The actual shape depends on how important it is to avoid delays.

6.3 Logistic Scenario

The scenario used for the evaluation of the context-aware routing in logistic networks is based on a topology that represents 18 cities in Germany and 35 major highway connections between them (70 if they are regarded as being unidirectional), as depicted in figure 6.2 and first introduced as a simulation scenario topology in [WGP05]. Each of the cities is a vertex in the scenario, and each vertex can be a source and a sink for goods.

The edge lengths in this scenario are given in table 6.1. The free fields in the table mean there is no edge that directly connects the corresponding vertices, i.e. only the connections that are visible in the depicted topology are represented in the table. If not stated differently, the maximum allowed speed on the edges is set to 100 km/tu, where tu is the unit of model time. Regarding the model time as being specified in hours would not be realistic when truck speeds are regarded, which usually are not allowed to drive at 100 km/h.

All vertices in the scenario have storage and transshipment capacities. The following costs are assigned to these capacities:

- unloading: 25 mu (monetary units) per ton
- loading: 25 mu per ton
- storage: 5 mu per ton and tu.

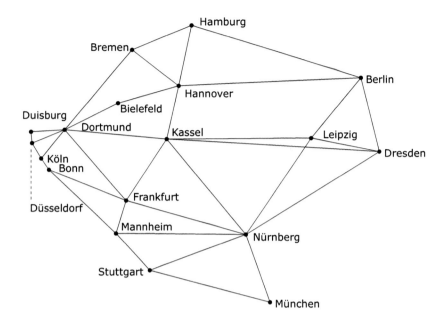

Figure 6.2: Logistic scenario topology [WGP05]

A vertex is not capable of unloading or loading several vehicles in parallel, so a vehicle has to wait when another vehicle is being (un)loaded.

Within the scenario, there is a predefined set of vehicles that are initially placed at some of the vertices. These vehicles are limited in their capacity and their speed. If not stated differently, the vehicles are characterised by following parameters:

- speed: 100 km/tu
- capacity: 12 tons (medium-sized truck)
- diesel consumption: 18 l/100 km plus 1 l/100 km for each ton of cargo (realistic estimate based on driver statements in Internet forums). The CO_2 output corresponds directly to the diesel consumption as for each litre of diesel per 100 km, the CO_2 output is 26.6 g/km. Slightly different values for the relation between diesel consumption and CO_2 emissions can also be found in literature and Internet resources, but the given value is the one used in official documents by the European Union, e.g. [otEC04].
- costs per km (fuel, wear etc.): 0.4 mu
- route planning hop limit: 3.

The goods are either generated during simulation runtime or specified in lists. Although they are called "packages" in the following, their dimensions are not necessarily small. The following parameters are assumed for the packages:

- dimension: 1 ton
- target budget: According to the shortest possible path length, 2 mu/km (e.g. if the shortest path length is 100 km, the target budget is 200 mu)
- delay fine: 10 mu/tu.

It has to be noted that several of these parameters, especially the cost-related parameters, are chosen arbitrarily, while others are based on realistic data (e.g. the diesel consumption and CO_2 output) or on experiences from previous simulations (e.g. the route planning hop limits). The topology itself is based on real locations and distances, and the vehicles' emission values are based on realistic values as well. The transport demand and the choice of the amount, capacity and location of vehicles, on the other hand, is done according to previous publications (e.g. [SRRWM08]) to achieve comparability to the results presented there.

6.3.1 Analytical Estimate of Routing Messages in the Scenario

In the given scenario, the number of vertices is $N = 18$, and the average node degree is $K = 70/18 = 3.\bar{8}$. Without any forwarding limitations, the equations 5.6 and 5.11 give estimates of

$$n_{paths,partial} = \sum_{i=1}^{17} \left[\frac{16!}{(17-i)!} \left(\frac{3.\bar{8}}{17} \right)^i \right] = 21306 \qquad (6.6)$$

package route replies and

$$n_{RREQs,partial} = \sum_{i=1}^{17} \left[n_{notinc,i} \frac{16!}{(17-i)!} \left(\frac{3.\bar{8}}{17} \right)^i \right] = 71620 \qquad (6.7)$$

route requests per package route discovery.

With a hop limit of 3, one vehicle route discovery generates estimated

$$n_{paths,partial} = 3.\bar{8}^3 = 58.813 \qquad (6.8)$$

vehicle route replies and

$$n_{RREQs,partial} = \sum_{i=1}^{3} 3.\bar{8}^i = 77.826 \qquad (6.9)$$

vehicle-initiated route request messages according to equation 5.15 and equation 5.16.

As for this graph, the topology is known, the amount of 3-hop vehicle paths can be determined directly with the help of the graph's adjacency matrix A. For each vertex the amount of outgoing paths of length 3 is the sum over the corresponding matrix row of A^3. This gives values between 36 (for the vertex "Duisburg" as starting vertex) and 142 (for the vertex "Nürnberg"). On average, each vertex has 76.6667 possible outgoing vehicle routes. This is more than the estimated value calculated above. The reason is that not all vertices have the same degree. Higher degrees have a significantly higher impact to the number of available paths than low node degrees, especially if several of them are adjacent (which holds for the vertices near the centre of the scenario).

These estimations already show quite clearly that the scalability problem mainly affects the package routing. To make it worse, not only does the single package routing generate nearly 3 orders of magnitude more messages, but there are also usually a lot more packages than vehicles in the network.

	Berlin	Hamburg	München	Köln	Frankfurt	Dortmund	Stuttgart	Düsseldorf	Bremen	Duisburg	Hannover	Nürnberg	Dresden	Leipzig	Bielefeld	Bonn	Mannheim	Kassel
Kassel					190	160					165	310	390	300				-
Mannheim					100		135					245				220	-	
Bonn				25	180											-	220	
Bielefeld						80					115				-			
Leipzig	160											255	120	-				300
Dresden	175											305	-	120				390
Nürnberg			175		200		210					-	305	255			245	310
Hannover	260	150							105		-				115			165
Duisburg						75		30		-								
Bremen		105				215			-		105							
Düsseldorf				50		60		-		30								
Stuttgart			230				-					210					135	
Dortmund				100	235	-		60	215	75					80			160
Frankfurt					-	235						200				180	100	190
Köln				-		100		50								25		
München			-				230					175						
Hamburg	280	-							105		150							
Berlin	-	280									260		175	160				

Table 6.1: Edge lengths (in km) in the given scenario topology

6.4 Logistic Simulation

6.4.1 Simulation Environment

The simulative evaluation in the logistic scenario is done using the "Logistics and Communication Simulator" (LoCoSim) that has been developed specifically for simulation of autonomous logistic processes [Com09]. This simulator is based on the Communication Networks Class Library (CNCL), which was originally developed at the RWTH Aachen and is now maintained by the Communication Networks group at the University of Bremen [Com08].

The LoCoSim simulator is a discrete-event simulator, so the simulation is controlled with the help of events that are sent and received by event handlers. These events represent the communication between participating entities as well as the logistic process. The main event handlers within the simulator are:

- vertices,
- edges,
- vehicles,
- packages,
- package generators.

Vertices   The vertices are fixed locations in the network. They provide functions for package storage, vehicle unloading and loading. Furthermore, they contain all functionality that is required for proper execution of the DLRP, i.e. the ability to handle and process route requests, route announcements and route disannouncements. To achieve this, the vertices have to handle communication events as well as logistic process events.

Edges   The edges are responsible for modelling the actual transport between vertices. A vertex hands over a departing vehicle to the respective edge by an event. The edge then controls the vehicle's travel time, and when the vehicle has completed its trip on the edge, it is handed over to the next vertex. As the edge itself is a representation of a physically passive component that does not communicate or make decisions, the edge event handling is also limited to events that model the transport process.

Vehicles   Vehicles are moving along the edges, carrying packages towards their destinations. The vehicles create and handle events related to the DLRP communication (route requests, route replies, route announcements, route disannouncements) and during loading and unloading at the vertices, they also handle logistic process events.

Packages and package generators   Packages can either be created at simulation runtime with the help of package generators, or they can be predefined in a list at the start of the simulation. Independent of how they are created, they are event handlers that handle logistic process events as well as DLRP communication events.

Package generators are creating packages. They are associated with vertices to where they send the created packages. So the generators are only handling logistic process events.

Simulation configuration   The simulation is configured with a set of XML-files. The main file contains the network's topology, i.e. information about the vertices and edges, and the specification of the vehicles that are present in the scenario. Additionally, it is supposed to contain the specifications for package generators if any generators are assumed to be present in the scenario.

If a predefined package constellation is used, the corresponding package list is specified in a separate file. In this case, package generators that are specified in the main file are deactivated so that only the packages defined in the package list appear in the simulation.

Statistic collection   In order to collect statistics while simulations are running, the simulator contains a "StatisticCollector" object. This object is an event handler as well, and it is capable of collecting statistics at regular intervals as well as event-induced statistics (e.g. triggered by package deliveries). These statistics are stored in a set of result files where they are available for post-simulative evaluation.

Some technical implementation details of this simulator have been published in [BWG05], and a comparison with an agent-based simulation system has shown that LoCoSim has advantages in several aspects of logistic simulations, especially in runtime performance [BWG+06].

6.4.2 Simulation Results

6.4.2.1 Proof of Concept

For the initial proof of concept, a simulation was run with 25000 packages which have origins and destinations among all vertices. Each possible source-destination pair is represented among the packages. On average, 23 packages were entering the simulation per time unit. The delivery time window was arbitrarily chosen to be 15 time units for each package, regardless of whether it has to travel a short or a long distance. Due to the lack of knowledge concerning the achievable travel times, the choice of the time window does not necessarily mean it can be fulfilled.

The dynamics in this scenario are limited to those that are induced by the appearance of goods. Traffic jams or other sources of dynamics are only introduced later.

The settings for the vehicle context criteria were as follows:

- **Monetary revenue**: This revenue consists of the price offered by packages minus the vehicle costs per km and delay fines, under the constraint that a delay fine for a package is not higher than its offered price (otherwise it will not be picked up). The monetary revenue is not handled as an absolute value (in that case, it would be an additive criterion as described in section 5.2.4) but as revenue per km to achieve fairness between short and long routes. The packages' offered prices depend on the urgency and on whether the vehicle is already carrying the package. This is presented in more detail when the package costs are discussed.

  Costs for storage and transshipment of packages are considered to be package costs, as they depend on the package's decisions. Therefore, they are not part of the costs and revenue that is relevant for the vehicle.

  During the route request forwarding phase, a lower bound of 0.01 is used for the scaled revenue, as the revenue may improve on following hops and a premature discarding of route requests should be avoided here. For positive revenues, the used scale is based on the error function of a normal distribution with mean μ_{rev} and variance σ_{rev}^2:

$$f_s(rev) = \frac{1}{2}\left(1 + \text{erf}\left(\frac{rev - \mu_{rev}}{\sigma_{rev}\sqrt{2}}\right)\right). \tag{6.10}$$

  This is done because a maximum revenue is not known then. The μ_{rev} can be regarded as a target value for the revenue, i.e. the vehicle tries to achieve this revenue or a revenue above it. σ_{rev} is chosen relatively high compared to μ_{rev}, so that the resulting curve is smooth. In the given scenario, the values are $\mu_{rev} = 5mu/km$ and $\sigma_{rev} = 2mu/km$.

  When the vehicle makes a route decision, the scaling is different: Negative revenues are scaled to 0, and a linear scale is used for positive revenue values with the highest revenue from the received route replies being scaled to 1:

$$f_s(rev) = \begin{cases} \frac{1}{rev_{max}} rev & \text{if } rev \geq 0 \\ 0 & \text{if } rev < 0. \end{cases} \tag{6.11}$$

- **Ecological impact**: This ecological impact is averaged over the complete route, based on the estimated vehicle utilisation on the hops. As already mentioned before, the carbon dioxide output is taken as measure for the ecological impact. Similar to the monetary revenue, it is not a pure additive criterion, but it is the impact per tonne kilometre. The scaling chosen here is

$$f_s(CO_2) = \frac{1}{2} \, \text{erfc} \left(\frac{CO_2 - 100g/tkm}{30g/tkm\sqrt{2}} \right). \tag{6.12}$$

- **Risk of revenue loss**: Here, the monetary revenue that was calculated for the current route is compared to historic values that the vertices have obtained from previous transports. Each vertex maintains statistics (mean and variance) about the revenue on outgoing links. These statistics are aggregated to mean and variance values for a route in propagating route requests, and the current calculated revenue is positioned on the cdf of these statistics (assuming that the revenues follow a normal distribution):

$$p_{revloss} = \frac{1}{2} \left(1 + \text{erf} \left(\frac{rev - \mu_{rev}}{\sigma_{rev}\sqrt{2}} \right) \right). \tag{6.13}$$

Figure 6.3 illustrates the equation for the probability of revenue loss. The solid vertical line is the mean μ_{rev} of the route revenue statistics, the dashed lines represent the interval that is limited by the standard deviation σ_{rev}.

The risk is a value between 0 and 1 but with 0 as the best and 1 as the worst value. The applied scaling should map a risk of 0 to a value of 1, and should be monotonically decreasing for an increasing risk. The scaling that was chosen for this simulation was

$$f_s(p_{revloss}) = \frac{1}{p_{revloss} + 1}. \tag{6.14}$$

It can be seen from the given scaling function that $f_s(p_{revloss})$ is always 0.5 or higher. What is important here is that it is never 0. This was done to prevent that a route which has been unbeneficial in the past is never chosen again.

- **Risk of ecological expectation underachievement** The ecological impact that is calculated for this route is compared to historic data here. Actually, the historic data contains only information on previous vehicle utilisations, but the emissions can be calculated from it.

For the vehicles' first routing in the beginning of the simulation, no route requests or route replies are dropped (no criterion-based forwarding limits are applied). Later on, route replies are not sent back if the discovered route is a route

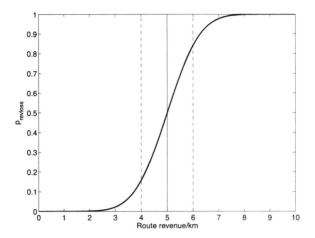

Figure 6.3: Revenue loss risk as a function of the expected route revenue with $\mu_{rev} = 5$ and $\sigma_{rev} = 1$

where the vehicle would remain completely empty. This is done by applying a limit for the ecological impact criterion, as the CO_2 emissions per tonne kilometre are infinite when the vehicle remains empty.

The packages' context criteria are handled as follows:

- **Route costs**: The package's route costs are an additive context criterion and consist of the price that is paid to the vehicles, the costs for storage and transshipment and the delivery fines that are to be paid if the package delivery is delayed with respect to the delivery time window. To explain the package's price offers, two things have to be mentioned first: 1. the packages have a target budget that depends on the distance between the origin and the destination (this was already stated before, see page 89), 2. depending on the urgency of delivery, which is considered to be the absolute difference between the currently expected delivery time and the due time, a package can have 3 urgency states, those are

    - TIME_EASY if they have 6 or more time units of buffer between the current expected delivery time and the due time,
    - TIME_TOUGH if they have 2 to 6 time units of buffer,
    - TIME_CRITICAL if they have less than 2 time units of buffer.

The price that the package offers to the vehicles for being transported is half of the unused target budget in the TIME_EASY state. When the state is TIME_TOUGH, the offered price is 75% of the unused budget, and in the TIME_CRITICAL state, it is 90% of the unused budget.

During the route discovery phase, only the transshipment, storage and delay costs are handled in the route request. The scaling used in the route discovery is adapted to that: When starting a route discovery, the package sets half of the unused target budget as the maximum cost, the scaling is linearly decreasing from 1 to 0 between 0 monetary units and the chosen maximum cost, and 0 above this limit. If the package experiences a timeout without having received a route reply, the budget most probably was too low, and the route discovery is restarted with a budget increase of 25 monetary units. This is repeated until either a route is found or a retry counter limit of 10 is reached.

When the package makes its route decision, it additionally compares the received route replies with the route of the vehicle with which it is currently travelling (only in case it is currently being transported, of course). If it finds that a route goes in the same direction as the vehicle's route, it realises that transshipment and storage costs can be saved by staying on the vehicle. As a consequence, it reduces the route costs by the costs for the saved transshipments and storage. Instead, it raises the offered price by a bonus of 20 mu for the current vehicle if this vehicle continues its planned route and keeps the package on board. This is done by specifying a "preferred vehicle" and the bonus for this vehicle as additional information in its route announcements. A short example can illustrate this: Assume a package has to travel from Hamburg to Frankfurt in the given scenario, and further assume that it is currently being transported towards Hannover. If the vehicle that is currently transporting the package intends to travel to Kassel next, the package realises that it is beneficial to continue its travel with this vehicle, because it can save 25 mu for unloading, 25 mu for loading and additional storage costs in Hannover. Therefore, it announces the current vehicle as preferred vehicle and shares 20 mu of its saved costs with the vehicle so that the vehicle also benefits from further transporting the package.

- **Risk of damage**: It is assumed that there are damage risks associated with transport, loading and unloading. They are dimensioned as follows:

  - Transport damage probability: $10^{-6}/km$
  - Unloading damage probability: $2 * 10^{-4}/unloading$
  - Loading damage probability: $10^{-4}/loading$

As it was not possible to obtain real-life reference data for this, the specified damage probabilities are chosen arbitrarily.

The risks are combined to an aggregate risk as described on page 86. This means the risk of damage is a multiplicative context criterion. For this proof-of-concept simulation, the maximum acceptable risk was set to 0.1 (which is quite high). The chosen scaling is therefore:

$$f_s(damagerisk) = \begin{cases} 1 - 10 * damagerisk & \text{if } 0 \leq damagerisk \leq 0.1 \\ 0 & \text{else} \end{cases}$$

(6.15)

- **Risk of delay**: Similar to the vehicle's risk of revenue loss, the package's risk of delay is based on historic values. Each vertex maintains statistics about how long packages are staying in storage, dependent on their next hop location. Together with estimated edge travel times (that depend on the edge speed), a ccdf for the expected total travel time can be created. The risk of delay is then determined based on this ccdf.

  The scaling applied for the risk of delay is following the same function as the vehicle's risk of revenue loss scaling, i.e.

$$f_s(p_{delay}) = \frac{1}{p_{delay} + 1}.$$

(6.16)

In the specified scaling, it is avoided that the scaled risk becomes 0. This is done as it may happen that the delay of a package is certain because it has been waiting for a pick-up too long. If the scaling would map this to 0, certainly delayed packages would never find an acceptable route any more, and thus never reach their destination.

In this simulation, all criteria were weighted equally with a weight of 1 with the only exception being the risk of ecological expectation underachievement which was weighted with 0, thus not influencing the decisions. This was done as the criterion was considered to be of minor importance, it was just included in the specification for the sake of completeness (so that there is a risk of underachievement for both the revenue and the ecological impact). The only forwarding limits applied are the budget limit used for the routing of packages, and a hop limit of 5 for package route requests.

Figure 6.4 shows the development of transport capacity utilisation over simulation time, determined in equidistant time intervals of 1 tu starting from the simulation initialisation until 1090 tu, which is shortly after the last out of 25000 packages enters the simulation. In the simulation run from which the displayed

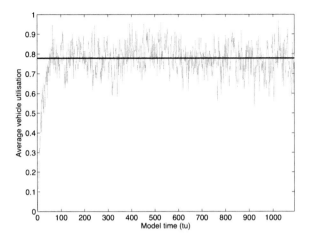

Figure 6.4: Vehicle capacity utilisation in the proof-of-concept simulation

graphs are taken (the first row of table C.1), 24295 packages were delivered at 1090 tu. It can be seen that there is a transient phase at the beginning of the simulation. In this phase, the first packages enter the simulation, and the initially empty vehicles collect their first loads. After that transient phase, the utilisation reaches a stable phase where it varies around an average utilisation value. The solid horizontal line marks this average value of 0.7783 for the vehicle utilisation between 50 and 1090 tu.

The convergence of the average utilisation can also be seen on the average CO_2 output graph shown in figure 6.5, as the output per tkm is directly related to the vehicle utilisation. It has to be noted that this graph shows the development of the overall average over time and vehicles, i.e. a point on the graph stands for the average over all vehicles and the time interval from the simulation start until the current point in time. It has to be noted that the CO_2 statistic is not just achieved by boosting the utilisation with unnecessary transports (see also the vehicle utilisation figures in comparison to the routing from [SRRWM08] shown on the following page).

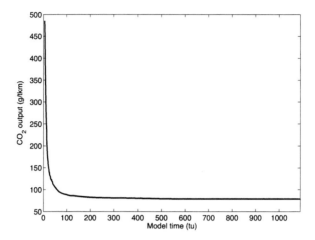

Figure 6.5: CO_2 output per tkm in the proof-of-concept simulation

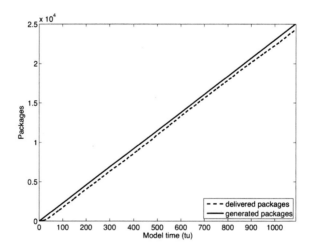

Figure 6.6: Generated and delivered packages in the proof-of-concept simulation

Figure 6.6 shows the cumulated amount of generated versus the cumulated amount of delivered packages during the simulation, so for each displayed point of model time, it can be identified how many packages were generated and how many were delivered up to that time. It can be seen that the lines are approximately parallel, which means the delivery rate matches the generation rate. The distance between the two lines with respect to the model time represents the time it takes in average from a package's generation to its delivery. Zooming closer into the diagram reveals that this time is a little higher than 20 tu (see figure 6.7). Recalling that it was specified in the simulation settings that the packages have 15 tu to be delivered in time, it becomes obvious that, although the pure delivery rate is high enough to be able to deliver as many packages as are being created, the timeliness of delivery cannot be achieved for a lot of packages. The histogram depicted in figure 6.8 illustrates this. Although there is also a significant portion of packages that are delivered on time, the average delay (delay being defined as the difference between due time and delivery time) is 10.6014 tu. This leads to the following consequences:

- Several packages exceed their target budget because they have to pay delay fees and because they increase their price offers towards the vehicles in order to get transported. Figure 6.9 provides a histogram of the costs in relation to the target budget. The average cost/budget relation is 1.0045 here, the median is still below 1 (it is 0.8693). A relation above 1 means that the budget is exceeded. The comparison of the average and the median relation, as well as the long tail of the histogram for relations above 1, shows that while the majority of packages can stay within their budget, some of them heavily exceed it.
- Due to the increased offers from the packages, the vehicles' revenue increases, as shown in figure 6.10. This is beneficial for the vehicles but certainly not for the packages.

To prove that the good vehicle capacity utilisation of 0.7783 is not just achieved by taking packages on unnecessarily long trips, the package routes were recorded and compared to the shortest possible routes. This comparison yielded an average relative distance of 1.3560, i.e. the package route length was, in average, 1.3560 times the shortest path length. Compared with the results in [SRRWM08] and [RMSR09], this puts the achieved results already in a good position in the evaluation chart proposed there. This can be seen from the comparison chart shown in figure 6.11. Table 6.2 explains in more detail which routing and decision concept is used for which point in the chart, and with which amount of logistic entities. For comparison, with the decision concept used in [SRRWM08] (and briefly de-

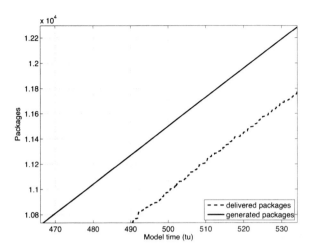

Figure 6.7: Generated and delivered packages in the proof-of-concept simulation, zoomed

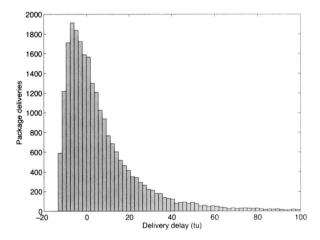

Figure 6.8: Histogram of package delays

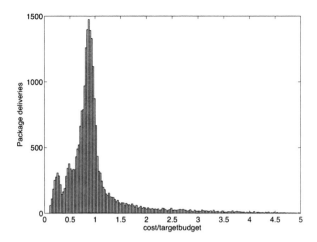

Figure 6.9: Histogram of package costs

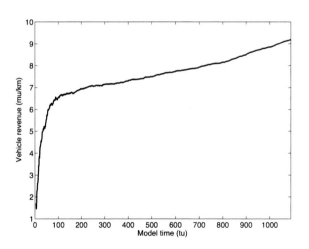

Figure 6.10: Average vehicle revenue in the proof-of-concept simulation

scribed in Appendix B) being used on this scenario for 25000 generated packages, the average relative distance is 1.9038, and the average vehicle capacity utilisation is 0.9449. This is also marked in figure 6.11. The result means that in the latter concept, the packages are carried around on significantly longer trips, causing the vehicles to be higher utilised but in fact causing an overload situation, i.e. the vehicles are unable to achieve a delivery rate that matches or exceeds the package generation rate. This overload can be seen in figure 6.12 where the line for the delivered packages gradually diverges from the lines for the generated packages and the delivered packages using the MCCD. While both decision concepts are on a similar level after 200 time units, there is approximately a factor of 2 in the delivery time when comparing the results of the two concepts after 1000 units of model time.

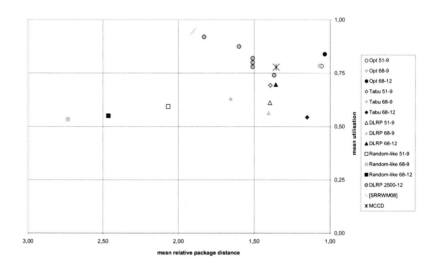

Figure 6.11: DLRP with MCCD result placed in the chart introduced in [RMSR09]. Result with decision concept from [SRRWM08] also displayed for comparison

Summing up the findings of the initial proof-of-concept simulation, it can be stated that the MCCD used here achieves stability with respect to the amount of goods being present in the scenario, as the delivery rate and the generation rate are approximately equal, and the vehicle utilisation also shows a constant range after the initial transient phase. It has to be noted that up to here, no weight optimisa-

Label	Packages	Vehicles	Routing concept
Opt 51-9	51	9	Optimal solution (CPLEX calculation)
Opt 68-9	68	9	Optimal solution (CPLEX calculation)
Opt 68-12	68	12	Optimal solution (CPLEX calculation)
Tabu 51-9	51	9	Tabu search
Tabu 68-9	68	9	Tabu search
Tabu 68-12	68	12	Tabu search
DLRP 51-9	51	9	DLRP decision concept [SRRWM08]
DLRP 68-9	68	9	DLRP decision concept [SRRWM08]
DLRP 68-12	68	12	DLRP decision concept [SRRWM08]
Random-like 51-9	51	9	Random assignment of packages to vehicles
Random-like 68-9	68	9	Random assignment of packages to vehicles
Random-like 68-12	68	12	Random assignment of packages to vehicles
DLRP 2500-12	2500	12	DLRP decision concept [SRRWM08] different random seeds
[SRRWM08]	25000	12	DLRP decision concept [SRRWM08]
MCCD	25000	12	DLRP, MCCD

Table 6.2: Supplementary table to explain results in figure 6.11

tions or other optimisations have been applied, so there is still some improvement potential expected.

The publications [SRRWM08] and [RMSR09] compare the DLRP routing approach with a conventional, centralised Tabu Search method and conclude that it

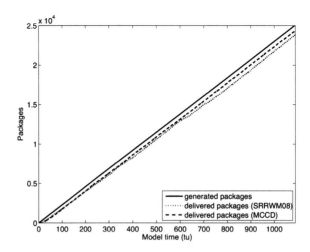

Figure 6.12: Generated and delivered packages in the simulation with decision concept from [SRRWM08] as comparison

shows competitive or better performance in the investigated scenario. As the use of the MCCD in DLRP leads to improvements according to the presented results, it can be deduced that the performance in comparison to conventional routing methods in logistic networks is good.

6.4.2.2 Weight Variations for Performance Improvement

As the initial simulation showed its major drawbacks in the fulfilment of time constraints, a counteraction that seems reasonable is to increase the weight of the package criterion "Risk of delay", so that high delay risks have a stronger impact. Simulations were run with weights for this risk ranging from 1 to 500, while all other configurations remained the same. The results are displayed in table 6.3. The column "Delivered packages" displays the amount of packages that were delivered in the observed time frame ($t \leq 1090$ tu). Note that while the previously shown results originate from one single simulation run, the results presented in the following are based on 10 simulation runs each, with different seeds being applied in the generation of packages (affecting the package's generation time, the origin and the destination). Results for the individual runs can be found in appendix C.

Weight	Mean delay	Median delay	Capacity utilisation	CO_2 (g/tkm)	Average relative distance	Package cost (mu/km)	Delivered packages
1.0	8.1349	1.9005	0.7710	79.1572	1.3416	1.9355	24399.1
2.0	7.9665	1.9511	0.7695	79.2426	1.3410	1.9458	24389.0
3.0	8.0272	1.9363	0.7681	79.3358	1.3355	1.9430	24375.6
4.0	8.0744	1.9604	0.7704	79.1861	1.3434	1.9552	24389.0
5.0	8.0693	2.0077	0.7699	79.2246	1.3448	1.9540	24365.0
25.0	8.1428	1.9678	0.7708	79.1555	1.3403	1.9576	24430.1
100.0	8.2444	2.0691	0.7710	79.1587	1.3371	1.9594	24389.2
500.0	8.1370	2.0754	0.7720	79.0762	1.3442	1.9529	24411.5

Table 6.3: Effect of different weights for the package delay risk

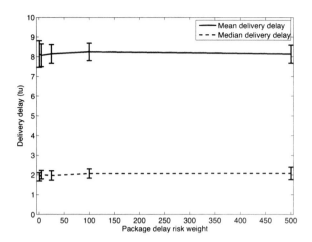

Figure 6.13: Mean and median delivery delays for different delay risk weights. Error bars represent the 95% confidence interval.

The results displayed in the table show no significant tendency of improvement achieved by the weight variation. This can also be seen from figure 6.13, where the mean and median delivery delays are shown including confidence intervals based on the sample standard deviation over 10 simulation runs for each of the displayed values. The shown confidence intervals are the intervals for 95% confidence, based on the Student-t distribution for 10 samples.

The use of confidence intervals based on the Student-t distribution is only correct if the samples follow this distribution, which represents samples from a normally distributed population in case of a small sample set. To check whether this assumption can be made, the Shapiro-Wilk test [SW65] for normality, respectively a Matlab implementation of this test, was applied to the samples. Resulting in values between 0.8483 and 0.9692 for the Shapiro-Wilk test statistic W, this test did not reject the normality hypothesis for any of the sample sets for the median delivery delays, so the assumption of a normal distribution is considered to hold here.

The lack of improvement by the weight variation can be explained with the help of figure 6.14: in the vast majority of route requests, a delay probability close to 1 is announced, which is due to the observed fact that the average deliveries take longer than the allowed delivery time window. Especially, the delay probability will not vary much for different routes from the same route discovery in most cases. All replies for one route discovery give a similar probability to be delayed, so they have very similar outcome for the criterion which was varied in weight here, and the variation of the weight does not have much impact on the route choice.

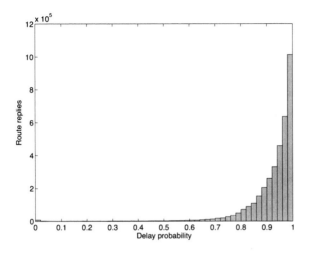

Figure 6.14: Delay risk announced to packages in route replies

The package costs are another criterion that is also influenced by delivery delays, as there are fines associated to the delay. In contrast to the delay risk, the costs are also influenced by how long the delay will be, as the fines are increasing with the delay. Therefore, another option is to vary the weight for the package costs. Table 6.4 and figure 6.15 show the corresponding results. The delay risk is weighted with a value of 1.0 here.

Here, the results are not much better than with varying weights for the delay risk. For weights from 1.0 to 25.0, the results are not even changing at all, which means the packages' decisions are then totally dominated by the other criteria. Only a high weight of above 250 gives better results for delays and costs, but less packages reach their destination in the observed time period in case of a weight of 750 or 990, so it cannot generally be stated that this high weight leads to better performance. Another effect that is visible is a decrease in the vehicle utilisation. A lower utilisation corresponds to a higher value of carbon dioxide emissions per tonne-kilometre, as the tonne-kilometres decrease.

Weight	Mean delay	Median delay	Capacity utilisation	CO_2 (g/tkm)	Average relative distance	Package cost (mu/km)	Delivered packages
1.0	8.1349	1.9005	0.7710	79.1572	1.3416	1.9355	24399.1
2.0	8.1349	1.9005	0.7710	79.1572	1.3416	1.9355	24399.1
5.0	8.1349	1.9005	0.7710	79.1572	1.3416	1.9355	24399.1
25.0	8.1349	1.9005	0.7710	79.1572	1.3416	1.9355	24399.1
100.0	8.0851	1.7533	0.7666	79.4355	1.3344	1.9691	24375.0
250.0	7.9719	1.7055	0.7667	79.4577	1.3470	1.9737	24346.1
500.0	6.5719	0.7741	0.7486	80.7127	1.3028	1.9216	24507.9
750.0	5.1082	0.2117	0.7228	82.6113	1.2546	1.8524	24200.7
990.0	4.1498	0.1901	0.7003	84.3737	1.2040	1.7754	23458.1

Table 6.4: Effect of different weights for the package costs

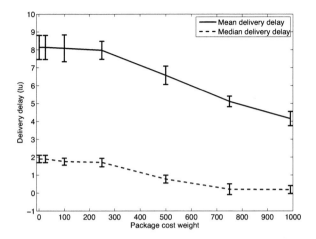

Figure 6.15: Mean and median delivery delays for different package cost weights. Error bars represent the 95% confidence interval.

Additionally, figure 6.16 shows that for a weight of 750, the system becomes unstable: the delivery times are gradually increasing as the model time progresses. So it can be said that among the weights that were simulated here, 500 gives the best performance with respect to delays, costs and amount of delivered packages.

What the results are indicating is that there is some but not too much potential for improvements concerning the delays. There are two possible reasons for this: Either the route evaluation function does not perform satisfactorily, or the time constraints in the scenario were chosen too small with the given transport demand and available vehicles. In the following, it is shown that the latter reason is causing the observed delays.

6.4.2.3 Modified Time Constraints

To examine whether the reason for the limited performance improvements with respect to the delivery delay is the evaluation function or the constraints in the scenario, the simulations were run again with varying time constraints. As the weight of 500 for the package costs showed the best results in the previous simulations, this weight configuration is kept while varying the length of the delivery

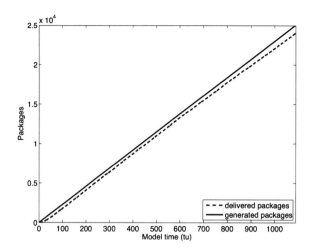

Figure 6.16: Generated and delivered packages with package cost weight of 750

time windows. Figure 6.17 shows the delivery delay cdfs for different delivery time windows, ranging from 15 to 40 time units.

What can be seen from the figure is that the cdf's shape is quite similar for each of the variations. For example, for a time window of 25 tu, a percentage of well above 70% of the packages are delivered within the time window. A large amount of those packages are even very early, which is also represented by the median of the distribution. What would now be desirable is to make the cdf steeper, i.e. while keeping the average delivery time, it would be beneficial if more packages are delivered in time (90% are a reasonable target value) while it would be acceptable if those packages that are early spend some more time.

For the following results, the delivery windows were now set to 25 tu, as this is a value in the range of the previous delivery window plus the average delay in the corresponding simulations. First, the weight for the delay risk was varied again, then the weight for the package costs.

The results for a varied weight of the delay risk, as displayed in table 6.5 again do not show much variation. The reason for this was already mentioned in the previous results: The delay risk usually is quite similar for different routes of a package, at least for the best of the available route options. There may be more route options which are worse with respect to the delay risk, but those are mostly

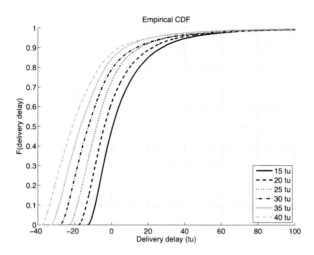

Figure 6.17: Cdf of delivery delays with different delivery time windows

longer and therefore also worse for the costs and damage risk, so that they are not chosen anyway.

As shown in table 6.6, when increasing the weight for the package costs, it can be seen that there is again no significant improvement for low weights, but for weights of 500 and above, a significant improvement of punctuality can be achieved. It has to be noted that while the delivery rate is still good for a weight of 750, it decreases for higher weights, which means there seems to be an optimum around this weight with respect to the delivery rate (which corresponds to stability) and the delay statistics.

Variations of vehicle weights were also examined but did not further improve the results. In contrast, there was a degradation visible when the vehicle's revenue weight was increased. A reduction of the vehicle's revenue weight did not markedly improve the results either.

These results shows two things: first, the evaluation function is working as intended, and second, the improvement potential in the scenario with more relaxed time constraints is higher, although the weights have to be chosen carefully to maintain stability.

Weight	Mean delay	Median delay	Capacity utilisation	CO_2 (g/tkm)	Average relative distance	Package cost (mu/km)	Delivered packages
1.0	-1.1508	-6.7926	0.7836	78.3134	1.3539	1.8310	24286.7
2.0	-0.9157	-6.8346	0.7836	78.3162	1.3533	1.8336	24307.9
3.0	-0.9185	-6.8259	0.7802	78.5304	1.3500	1.8242	24206.6
4.0	-1.0351	-6.8091	0.7801	78.5224	1.3444	1.8224	24290.6
5.0	-1.2307	-6.8123	0.7796	78.5778	1.3374	1.8133	24360.3
25.0	-1.1122	-6.8662	0.7781	78.6820	1.3408	1.8227	24306.9
100.0	-1.2637	-6.7884	0.7797	78.5674	1.3408	1.8103	24367.2
500.0	-1.2292	-6.7071	0.7791	78.5898	1.3456	1.8160	24332.1

Table 6.5: Effect of different weights for the package delay risk with more relaxed delivery time window

Weight	Mean delay	Median delay	Capacity utilisation	CO_2 (g/tkm)	Average relative distance	Package cost (mu/km)	Delivered packages
1.0	-1.1508	-6.7926	0.7836	78.3134	1.3539	1.8310	24286.7
25.0	-1.1508	-6.7926	0.7836	78.3134	1.3539	1.8310	24286.7
100.0	-0.7541	-6.6483	0.7837	78.3207	1.3526	1.8255	24287.8
250.0	-1.4673	-6.8295	0.7800	78.5459	1.3454	1.7965	24458.5
500.0	-3.2270	-8.1048	0.7592	79.9097	1.3188	1.7308	24445.9
750.0	-4.8878	-8.7632	0.7349	81.6667	1.2688	1.6195	24258.5
1000.0	-6.3828	-9.3196	0.6988	84.4809	1.1943	1.4844	23604.3
1500.0	-8.4308	-10.2143	0.5583	98.5810	1.1196	1.2663	19111.9

Table 6.6: Effect of different weights for the package costs with more relaxed time constraints

6.4.2.4 Forwarding Limit Variations

To evaluate the influence of Route Request forwarding limits on the amount of messaging as well as on the logistic performance, simulations were run with different limits. One of the applied limitation methods is the use of hop limits both in vehicle and goods routing. The hop limits applied to the earlier simulations were 3 hops for the vehicles' route requests and 5 hops for the packages' route requests. Now these limits are varied, and the results are shown in tables 6.7 and 6.8 (as before, for up to 1090 tu of model time). It has to be noted that the drop rates in these tables only include route requests dropped due to exceeded context criteria limits, not due to hop limits. This means the vehicle route request drops are only caused by negative revenues, the package route request drops by exceeded cost limits.

Hop limit	Mean delay	Capacity utilisation	Avg. rel. distance	Delivered packages	Total vehicle RREQs	Vehicle RREQ drop rate
1	1.5062	0.7158	1.3077	22562.7	40125	0
2	-2.8679	0.7650	1.3371	24365.4	206255	0.00760
3	-3.2270	0.7592	1.3188	24445.9	929385	0.00518
4	-3.6336	0.7555	1.2949	24539.2	3912147	0.00268

Table 6.7: Different hop limits for vehicle route requests (package hop limit: 5)

Hop limit	Mean delay	Capacity utilisation	Avg. rel. distance	Delivered packages	Total package RREQs	Package RREQ drop rate
3	-6.3706	0.6214	1.3094	21843.9	$3.50 \cdot 10^7$	0.3600
4	-3.4942	0.7534	1.3019	24492.5	$6.98 \cdot 10^7$	0.4590
5	-3.2270	0.7592	1.3188	24445.9	$8.71 \cdot 10^7$	0.5276
6	-2.8380	0.7612	1.3116	24433.0	$1.02 \cdot 10^8$	0.5560
7	-2.8129	0.7632	1.3150	24469.6	$1.08 \cdot 10^8$	0.5658

Table 6.8: Different hop limits for package route requests (vehicle hop limit: 3)

Interestingly, the results show that at some point, a further increase of the hop count limit does not lead to better performance, it just increases the routing traffic.

In the current setup, this limit is already reached with 2 hops for the vehicle routing and 4 hops for the package routing. 4 hops is also the hop count with which it is always possible to reach any other node in the current scenario. This is also the reason why 3 hops are not sufficient for package routing: Some source-destination pairs are more than 3 hops apart from each other.

The combination of a 2-hop limit for vehicle routing and a 4-hop limit for package routing leads to the following results.

- Mean delay: -3.4134 tu
- Avg. rel. distance: 1.3262
- Capacity utilisation: 0.7598
- Delivered packages: 24477.1
- Total veh. RREQs: 205868
- Total pack. RREQs: 66294573
- Veh. RREQ drop rate: 0.00700
- Pack. RREQ drop rate: 0.4660

According to these results, this combination is the optimal choice for the scenario. It has to be noted that the necessary hop count for packages depends on the scale of the logistic network, as the packages must be able to find a route to their destination. So, the minimum hop count that can be set for package route requests is the network diameter. Similarly, the vehicle routes must also be long enough to ensure that packages will be picked up. Therefore, the required hop count for the vehicles also depends on the network size.

Another observation that can be made here is the relation between the vehicle-induced routing traffic and the package-induced routing traffic. The package-induced traffic is much higher, although a significant portion of requests is dropped (i.e. not forwarded).

There are two components that influence the package route request drop rate: the maximum hop count and the limit on the package costs. To achieve a further reduction of package routing traffic, variations of this limit on the package costs are to be investigated. Without any limit on the package context criteria and a hop limit of 5, the amount of package route requests increases drastically to $5.96 * 10^9$ within the observed model time, which is nearly two magnitudes higher than with the previously applied limit, which was 50% of the remaining target budget plus an increase of 25 monetary units if a rediscovery is required (i.e. no route reply was received before a timeout occurred). The logistic performance decreases when there is no limit. The reason is that the applied scaling is calibrated for a maximum budget, i.e. it is 0 for costs above the budget. When there is only a hop limit but no other limit, there are many routes where the scaled cost criterion (and thus the complete route) is evaluated to 0, but still the corresponding route discovery is continued.

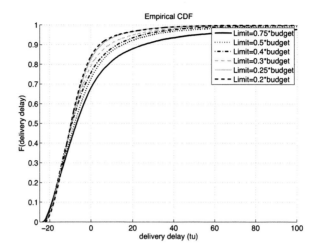

Figure 6.18: Delivery delay cdfs with varying forwarding limit for package costs

Simulations with different limits on the package costs showed an interesting result: not only is the amount of package route requests reduced with tighter limits, but as it can be seen from Figure 6.18, the delivery statistics improve as well when the limits are tighter. This matches the aforementioned observation that the performance decreases when no limit is applied. However, when the limits are further reduced below the levels shown in the diagram, the overall amount of deliveries decreases, which can be seen from the values in table 6.9, while the amount of route requests is not reduced much further. The graph in figure 6.19 shows that there is a minimum of transmitted route requests per successfully delivered package when the package cost limit is at 25% of the remaining target budget. The existence of this minimum matches what was stated in section 5.2.5: Too strict limits can cause more rediscoveries and thus lead to an increase in route discovery traffic.

Cost limit (% of budget)	Mean delay	Capacity utilisation	CO_2 (g/tkm)	Avg. rel. distance	Delivered packages	Total pack. RREQs	Pack. RREQ drop rate
10	-8.6105	0.4904	108.3365	1.1903	19389.1	14093143	0.7192
15	-7.5644	0.6276	90.8233	1.2145	22593.2	18536186	0.7078
20	-7.2476	0.6892	85.1759	1.2445	23907.8	19293375	0.7014
25	-7.5575	0.6982	84.4483	1.2350	24404.2	18778755	0.6929
30	-6.8387	0.7127	83.3221	1.2578	24406.8	24174710	0.6723
40	-5.1410	0.7344	81.6990	1.2762	24527.8	53992792	0.6060
50	-3.2270	0.7592	79.9097	1.3188	24445.9	87145728	0.5276
75	0.4210	0.7873	78.0588	1.3758	23978.6	181872783	0.3487

Table 6.9: Different cost limits for package route requests

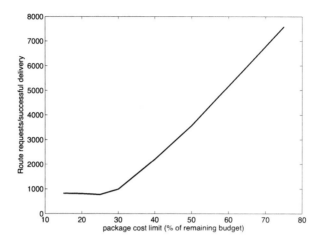

Figure 6.19: Transmitted route requests per successfully delivered package

These results can be explained as follows: The packages' decision process takes place after either the expiration of a timeout or the reception of a fixed amount of route replies. The latter is the cause for the improvements with tighter limits: Loose limits for route request forwarding lead to more incoming route replies at the package, and consequently a higher amount of lower quality routes. As the sequence of the route reply arrivals does not directly correspond to the route quality, a higher amount of low quality routes increases the probability that the route reply count has already reached the decision-initiating threshold before the best route replies arrive, thus leading to the choice of a suboptimal route. If the limits are too strict, some packages fail finding a route, which is the cause for the decreased overall amount of deliveries in that case. More frequent route discovery retries prevent a further significant improvement with respect to the route requests being generated.

To combine the benefits of optimised hop count limits and package cost limits and validate whether the individual optima also produce a good result when combined, simulations were run with a vehicle route hop limit of 2, a package route hop limit of 4 and a package cost limit of 25 % of the remaining budget. The following listing shows the results:

- Mean delay: -7.7341 tu
- Avg. rel. distance: 1.2580
- Capacity utilisation: 0.7055
- Delivered packages: 24283.1
- Total veh. RREQs: 194701
- Total pack. RREQs: 17854845
- Veh. RREQ drop rate: 0.01452
- Pack. RREQ drop rate: 0.6916

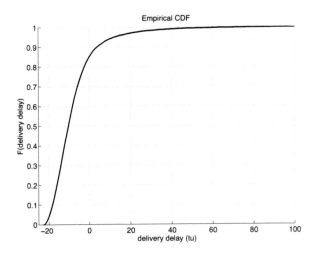

Figure 6.20: Delivery delay cdf for optimised forwarding limits

It can be seen that while the route requests being sent in the network are significantly reduced both for vehicle and package initiated requests, the logistic performance is still good, which can also be seen from figure 6.20 which depicts the delivery delay CDF. This shows that optima from different forwarding limitation approaches can be combined to achieve a solution that performs better than the individual optima alone.

6.4.2.5 Traffic Jams

In the simulations presented up to here, the only source of dynamics was the generation of transport demand. This is now extended by simulations that include randomly occurring traffic jams. The following results are obtained through simulations with traffic jams occurring randomly on the edges between the locations "Dortmund", "Kassel" and "Frankfurt", which are among the most used edges in the scenario. A jam probability of 0.25 here means that in average, the edge is jammed 25 % of the time. The duration of a traffic jam is 0.5 time units. During a traffic jam, the speed on the edge is reduced to 10 % of the normal speed. The effective average speed on the links under presence of traffic jams with this speed reduction is

$$v_{eff} = (1 - 0.9 p_{jam}) v_{max}. \tag{6.17}$$

The simulations are run in two variations: the first one is that the vertices are not aware of the traffic jams and determine expected travel times only based on the allowed speed and the edge length. In the second variation, vertices maintain statistical data on the vehicles' travel times and use the effective average speed in their context determination instead of the allowed speed. Thereby, the travel time estimates are more accurate.

Jam prob.	Mean delay	Median delay	Capacity utilisation	Avg. rel. distance	Package cost (mu/km)	Delivered packages
0	-3.2270	-8.1048	0.7592	1.3188	1.7308	24445.9
0.1	-2.3702	-7.4612	0.7781	1.3135	1.7753	24426.5
0.25	-0.6042	-6.9609	0.8028	1.2882	1.8451	24281.6
0.5	3.7035	-5.6895	0.8475	1.2443	1.9773	23293.5
0.75	16.6789	-4.7430	0.8633	1.1973	2.3204	21142.4

Table 6.10: Influence of traffic jams on the performance (without travel time statistics)

The results displayed here do not show significant differences between the cases where the vertices are aware of the traffic jams and those where they have no knowledge about them. This has to do with the topology that is used here: Especially the alternatives to the links Frankfurt-Kassel and Kassel-Dortmund require large detours, so that they are only favourable if the effective speed on the jam-affected links is very low. Due to this, not many detours are taken.

Jam prob.	Mean delay	Median delay	Capacity utilisation	Avg. rel. distance	Package cost (mu/km)	Delivered packages
0	-3.3783	-8.0267	0.7596	1.3118	1.7262	24504.5
0.1	-2.3104	-7.8456	0.7704	1.3010	1.7753	24382.9
0.25	-0.7525	-7.1847	0.7884	1.2710	1.8413	24299.2
0.5	3.9806	-6.1462	0.8358	1.2426	2.0252	23138.4
0.75	13.0227	-5.4090	0.8430	1.1981	2.2637	21002.8

Table 6.11: Influence of traffic jams on the performance (with travel time statistics)

6.5 Summary of this Chapter

This chapter has presented the application of DLRP, the specialisation of the generic context-aware routing concept for routing of autonomous logistic entities (vehicles and packages). As the decision component of the concept, the MCCD was used in the logistic entities. It was shown that the complete concept, i.e. the combination of DLRP and MCCD, achieves good results in the investigated scenarios. Further, it could be shown that a properly conducted route request limitation, which was analytically discussed in chapter 5, can significantly reduce the communication traffic without negative influences to the logistic performance.

Therefore, the context-based routing framework in conjunction with the MCCD as the applied decision concept has proven to be applicable to distributed routing in transport logistics. The logistics-specific implementation of this concept, the DLRP, has shown good performance in the investigated scenarios, and it was also shown that the combination of MCCD and DLRP performs better than the DLRP in combination with other decision systems.

7 Evaluation in Wireless Sensor Networks

7.1 Evaluation Criteria for Sensor Networks

The relevant criteria in wireless sensor networks are related to the communication and to the fulfilment of the sensing task. Both are closely related, so that a good communication performance is required to fulfil the sensing task acceptably. For the sensing task, it is relevant that the network has a long lifetime, which means the energy consumption is low. As the communication consumes a significant amount of sensor energy, optimising the energy spent in communication usually means energy optimisation for the sensor network as a whole.

Furthermore, reactivity is relevant in cases where fast reactions to critical sensor values are required. This means the communication delays have to be low. Reliability of data delivery is another performance indicator, so the packet loss rate should be minimised.

7.2 Decision System Setup for Sensor Networks

In sensor network scenarios, particular attention is usually on network efficiency and reliability. This is the same here, so the following criteria are chosen for the MCCD:

- Node health
- Signal quality
- Route length.

The criteria are now discussed in detail.

Node health The node health is a reliability measure that denotes whether a node (or multiple nodes) on a route is expected to fail or not. The health can be based on the nodes' residual energy, but in hostile environments some of the sensed phenomena may also endanger the node. This is especially the case if the nodes are deployed in an environment where they have to detect disasters [WPTGG08]. The node health is a parameter with clearly defined upper and lower bounds. The lower bound is reached when either the node does not have any energy left or it is destroyed. This can be represented by a health value of 0. If the node has reached this health value, it obviously does not participate in the network any more. The upper bound means having full energy and not being exposed to a destruction threat. This full health status is represented by the value of 1. So the health is already in the range $[0, 1]$, with 1 being the best value, which means it can be used directly in the MCCD without applying a scaling function (or in other words, the scaling function is a multiplication with 1).

Signal quality The signal quality denotes whether a route is reliable with respect to minimisation of transmission failures that are caused by low signal strength or high interference. An indicator for the signal quality can be the *Received Signal Strength Indicator* (RSSI) which is usually given in dBW or dBm. It is a measure of the power with which the signal was received, and it is bounded at the lower end by the receiver sensitivity (which is usually somewhere around -90 dBm, e.g. it is typically -95 dBm for the Texas Instruments/Chipcon CC2420 chipset [Tex07] which is a popular chipset among sensor node manufacturers) and at the upper end by the maximum transmission power, which is typically 0 dBm for the aforementioned chipset. Note that according to the datasheet of this chipset, the typical maximum input level for the receiver is 10 dBm, so it can handle incoming transmissions with the maximum power. If the RSSI is used as the sole indicator for the signal quality, the scaling function to be chosen can be one that gives a value of 0 for the lowest quality and a value of 1 for the highest. It can be a linear scaling, but any other function that fulfils this requirement is also possible. If the receiver sensitivity is not known or not assumed to be present, the RSSI value range is open-ended at the lower side. In this case, the scaling function has to reflect this, which makes a function that asymptotically approaches 0 for negative RSSI values more appropriate.

Another signal quality indicator can be the *Signal to Interference and Noise Ratio* (SINR) which indicates the relation of the signal power to the power of any disturbing effects. This measure is usually given in dB, and it theoretically does not have a minimum or maximum. If this is used, a scaling function that approaches 0 for low SINR and that approaches 1 for high SINR should be chosen.

Route length The route length basically is the number of hops that the route includes. If all nodes use the same power level to transmit, optimising the route length implicitly includes an energy optimisation in the network, as less hops mean less nodes have to spend energy. Without the use of individual power control on the nodes, this equals to a reduction of the overall consumed energy. As the route length does not have an upper limit other than the total number of nodes in the networks (which is most probably unknown to the individual nodes), a scaling function that asymptotically approaches 0 for long routes is to be chosen here, for example a negative exponential function.

7.3 Sensor Network Scenario

For the sensor network simulation, a scenario was used which represents a case where the environment can threaten the sensor nodes. So this scenario is a good use case for an Environmental Monitoring-Aware (EMA) routing protocol. It is a forest fire scenario where 20 sensor nodes are randomly distributed over a forest area of 10x10 km as depicted in figure 7.1, with one sink at a corner of the area (the node labelled "sink_0"). This sink is receiving the sensor measurements. All other nodes are identical in that they each have the same sensing, computation and communication capabilities. Temperature sensing is among these capabilities. This scenario has already been used for the Proactive EMA protocol ([WPTGG08], [WPTGG09]) which is described in appendix chapter A.

It is simulated that a fire breaks out in the area 20 minutes after the start of the simulation, which on one hand is a phenomenon that the sensors should detect and on the other hand threatens the sensors to be destroyed. The fire spreads over the area in an elliptic fashion according to the ellipse shown in the figure, with a spreading speed of 1 m/s on the minor axis and 2 m/s on major axis of the ellipse. Actually, this spread is faster than a usual forest fire spread (in [SAW$^+$04], spread speeds of up to 70 m/min were observed for crown fires), so it can be considered a worst case spread which requires maximum reactivity in the network.

The applied temperature model is simple: As long as a node is not exposed to fire, its temperature values are normally distributed with a mean of 20 degrees Celsius and a variance of one degree Celsius. When the node becomes exposed to the fire, a linearly growing offset is added to the node's temperature value. Figure 7.2 shows the temperature curve at sensor node 1, a node that is located close to the fire break out location. It can be clearly seen that in the applied temperature model, the temperature increases quickly when the fire reaches the node, which in the illustrated case happens at ca. 1900 seconds of model time. Within a short time, the maximum temperature threshold is reached and the node is destroyed.

The nodes measure the temperature every 15 seconds and transmit the obtained values to the base station as input into a forest fire detection algorithm and fire fighter alerting. Each node has an individual starting time for its first measurement

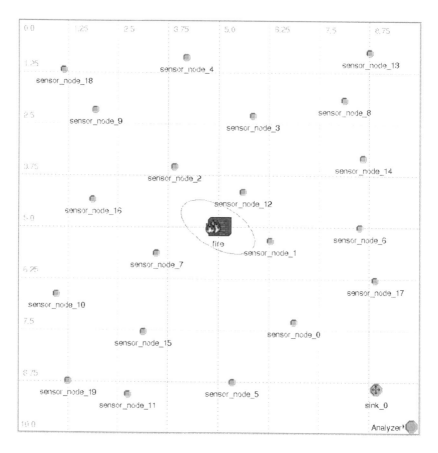

Figure 7.1: Sensor network scenario layout [WPTGG08], [WPTGG09]

to avoid effects caused by synchronous transmissions of all nodes. Assuming that the temperature is not the only data that a node is sending, the measured values are part of a data packet of 1 kbit size. This means each node is transmitting 1 kbit every 15 seconds, resulting in an overall rate of generated data at all nodes of 1.33 kbit/s or 1.33 packets/s.

The transmission power, which is equal for all nodes in the scenario, is chosen to be 1 mW (=0 dBm) so that multiple hops are required to reach the sink. Only the four nodes that are closest to the sink are in direct communication range with it. It has to be noted that in this specific scenario, the receiver sensitivity is not set, so

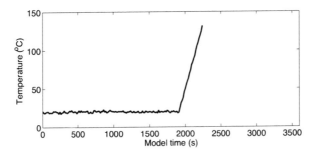

Figure 7.2: Temperature at sensor node 1

that signal strength levels below -95 dBm (=-125 dBW) are also possible. Without a receiver sensitivity being set, the radio model being used in the simulation allows that a signal is detected at RSSI levels of around -143 dBW, with a high error rate due to the influence of noise (see also [Luk07], chapter 5). This error rate becomes less with increased RSSI.

This scenario and variations thereof are used here for evaluation.

7.4 Sensor Network Simulation

7.4.1 Simulation Environment

For the evaluation in the wireless sensor network scenario, the simulation tool OP-NET Modeler [OPN08] is used. The sensor node models are based on version 1.0 of the Open-ZB [OZ08] implementation of the physical and data link layers defined in the IEEE 802.15.4 [IEE03] standard. Above the data link layer, a network layer is placed that utilises the context-aware routing protocol that is presented in this thesis. An application layer that models the sensor data generation and the data sink completes the node model, as it can be seen in figure 7.3.

The Open-ZB implementation was changed in the data link layer from beacon-enabled mode with PAN coordinator to ad-hoc mode as part of a master thesis work [Luk07], [WLTG+08] to enable multihop paths and node-to-node communication. These changed layers were also used in [WPTGG08] and [WPTGG09].

As the network layer has to use the MCCD routing, it was implemented according to that. The implementation consists of two processes: a main process that covers most of the tasks such as sending and receiving data, initiating routing and

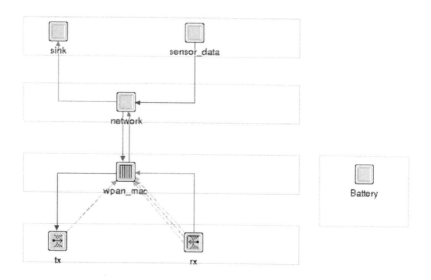

Figure 7.3: Sensor node model

choosing routes, and a subprocess that handles incoming route requests. These processes are depicted in figures 7.4 and 7.5.

Comparing the depicted process models with the general state models in figures 3.2 and 3.3, there are only small differences (e.g. the existence of init states), the operation follows the general model.

7.4.2 Simulation Results

The initial WSN simulations are performed on the scenario described above. For the context criteria, the settings are described in the following.

Node health   Within this scenario, the nodes' residual energy is not of high importance due to the spread of the fire that eliminates the nodes earlier. Therefore, only the sensed temperature, which indicates the threat level of the node, is taken into account for the node health. Temperatures below 30 degrees are considered normal, so the node health is 1 for those, and between 30 and 130 degrees, the node health is linearly decreasing to 0. At higher temperatures, the node is destroyed.

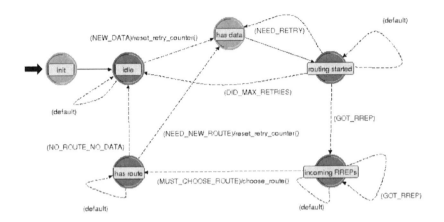

Figure 7.4: Network layer process model

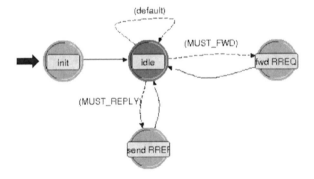

Figure 7.5: Network layer RREQ handling subprocess model

As already discussed previously, the health values are used directly, i.e. without any further scaling.

Signal quality The RSSI value is used as a measure for the signal quality. In the initial simulation, no limitation that is induced by the receiver sensitivity is assumed, so theoretically, there is no lower limit for the RSSI. Due to this, a scaling function that asymptotically approaches 0 for low RSSI values is utilised:

$$f_s(RSSI) = e^{\frac{RSSI}{50}}.$$ (7.1)

The 50 in this scaling is chosen according to the usual value range of the RSSI for IEEE 802.15.4 sensor nodes.

Route length   For the route length, which equals the hop count, a negative exponential scaling is chosen, i.e.

$$f_s(hopcount) = e^{-hopcount}.$$ (7.2)

These choices for the criteria are the same as for the Proactive EMA approach presented in [WPTGG08] and described in appendix A. This allows a direct comparison of the same decision function in a proactive and a reactive EMA routing approach in the same scenario.

7.4.2.1 Initial Results

Initially, the reactive routing approach was implemented as described and simulated with the following settings:

- Hop count limit: 7 Hops
- RSSI limit: -143 dBW
- Routing timeout: 0.1 seconds
- Route lifetime: 30 seconds
- Scenario settings as described in section 7.3 and used in [WPTGG08]

Additionally, one further method of routing traffic limitation is applied: If a route request reaches a node which has recently done a route detection and selection itself, so that it has a route to a sink, it only unicasts the new route request along the existing route, instead of broadcasting it.

Figure 7.6 shows the generation and delivery rate over the simulation. This only includes sensor data packets, no routing overhead. The rates are average values for a time window of 250 seconds (moving average values), which makes it easier to identify how close the generation and delivery rates are, but it also smoothens delivery rate breakdowns, which happen for example at a model time of around 3700 s and 4800 s. Still, the breakdowns remain clearly visible.

The cause for the breakdown at around 3700 s is the failure of sensor_node_17 and sensor_node_6, which fail in short sequence and thereby make the sink inaccessible for the remaining sensor nodes in the upper right part of the area. The

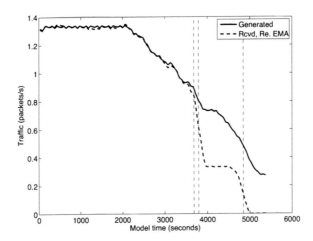

Figure 7.6: Data delivered at the sink with Reactive EMA, dashed vertical lines: failures of nodes 17, 6, 5 (from left to right)

first two dashed vertical lines show exactly when these failures occur. Similarly, the failure of sensor_node_5 at around 4800 s indicated by the third dashed line breaks the last remaining link to the sink, thus isolating the sink from the remaining active sensor nodes. Before these breakdowns occur, the curve for the delivered data largely follows the one for the generated data, that means the protocol performs well in terms of reliable data delivery as long as there is a possible route to the sink.

Figure 7.7 shows the histogram of the end-to-end delays that are between 0.0 s and 1.0 s with Reactive EMA. In this histogram, the 0.1 s routing timeout can be clearly seen in the peak that appears slightly above 0.1 s. Generally, the delays are well below one second (except for a few single values that are higher, see figure 7.8). Given the granularity of measurements (and transmissions), which is 1 measurement per 15 seconds, these delays can generally be considered as being good enough as they are low compared to the measurement interval.

Figure 7.9 shows the overall energy consumption for communication. This is the energy the transceivers spend for transmission and reception of data. Energy that is required for processing is not considered here. The graph shows the cumulative sum of energy that is spent. In the comparative evaluation against other routing methods which is presented in the following pages, it is shown how these values

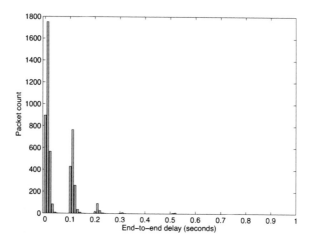

Figure 7.7: Histogram of end-to-end delays with Reactive EMA

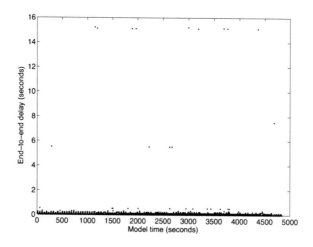

Figure 7.8: End-to-end delays with Reactive EMA

(the energy consumption as well as the end-to-end delays) have to be put into relation.

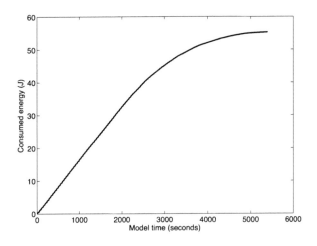

Figure 7.9: Energy consumption for communication in Reactive EMA

7.4.2.2 Comparison to other Routing Approaches

To evaluate the Reactive EMA protocol, its performance is compared to other pro-tocols. One of the protocols used for comparison is AODV (see also section 2.1 for a short description). This well-known reactive routing protocol has its origins in IEEE 802.11 wireless LANs, but it also exists in implementations for wireless sensor networks, for example as TinyAODV [Tin] for the TinyOS [Tin08] sensor operating system. AODV is chosen as a representative for conventional reactive routing approaches that do not use context information for their route decision but only decide based on the hop count.

Apart from the comparison of Reactive EMA against the also reactive AODV, it is also compared against proactive protocols. OLSR is chosen as a well-known conventional proactive protocol. Proactive EMA, which was introduced in [WPTGG08] and is described in appendix A, is chosen as a second proactive pro-tocol to compare with. This provides a direct comparison of the proactive and reactive implementation of the EMA idea.

Comparison to AODV   In the simulation model used here, the AODV enabled nodes are consisting of 802.15.4 lower layers (which are the same as used for Reactive EMA) and the "normal" Opnet implementation of AODV in the network layer which is usually used in conjunction with 802.11 lower layers. To achieve comparability in the results, the route lifetime was set to 30 seconds in AODV as well. As in AODV, the route lifetime depends on the allowed hello loss, the hello interval was set to 15 seconds and the allowed hello loss to 2 messages.

The results depicted in 7.10 show that AODV fails in delivering all data to the sink when all nodes are alive.

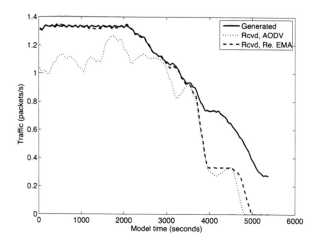

Figure 7.10: Data delivered at the sink, AODV vs. Reactive EMA

The reason for the poor AODV delivery rate originates from the combination of general AODV behaviour and implementation-specific details: As the AODV protocol does not take signal strength values into account when selecting a route, it in some cases selects routes with a low signal strength, just because they have a lower hop count. Those routes are obviously more prone to transmission errors than routes with a high signal strength. The preference of routes with a low hop count adds up to this issue as a low hop count in average means a larger distance between the nodes and therefore again a lower received signal strength.

The MAC layer of a node will usually try to retransmit upon a failure until a retry limit is reached. The default value for this limit (*macMaxFrameRetries*) is defined to be 3 in the IEEE 802.15.4 standard [IEE03], so it is reached quickly. When it is reached, the MAC layer drops the frame. The implemented Node model does not use link layer acknowledgements between the MAC and the Network layer, so it is not indicated to the AODV module in the network layer that the transmission failed. The AODV module only detects link failures by missing Hello messages, and as those Hello messages are usually much shorter than user data packets, their transmission is less likely to fail due to bit errors. As a consequence, the AODV module does not recognise that a link is problematic as long as the Hello messages are there, so the node continues using the link and loses packets from time to time.

The non-existence of link layer acknowledgements is an issue that is present in some sensor network operating systems, such as TinyOS 1.0, therefore it can be considered a valid assumption. Sensor nodes operating an AODV protocol on TinyOS 1.0 in practice also have to rely only on Hello messages to determine whether a link is fine or not.

While the Reactive EMA also does not make use of link layer acknowledge-ments and therefore can also not react directly to transmission failures, the results show a much better success rate. This can be explained by the fact that Reactive EMA uses more context information, especially the use of RSSI values can lead to routes with better robustness with respect to transmission errors.

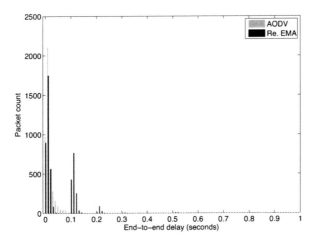

Figure 7.11: End-to-end delay histogram for AODV and Reactive EMA

The end-to-end delays depicted in figure 7.11 show that AODV is generally a bit faster, which is an expected result as AODV can immediately start sending when it has received a route reply, while Reactive EMA waits for multiple incoming route replies from which it then selects a route. This makes Reactive EMA wait for a longer time, especially in cases when it does not receive many route replies and the routing timeout is expiring before a route is selected. But as stated before, the delays are generally very low in comparison to the measurement interval in this scenario, so they are of minor importance here.

A result that is better than expected is shown in figure 7.12: The energy consumption in Reactive EMA is lower. Although AODV only processes the first incoming route request and neglects later incoming route requests from the same route discovery, while a Reactive EMA node may forward multiple route requests per discovery, Reactive EMA succeeds in keeping control over the route discovery traffic. This shows that the applied *flood limiting* works well. Additionally, the aforementioned problem with low quality routes in AODV also has some influence here: The higher loss probability in AODV causes more retransmissions, which contribute to the overall power consumption in the network.

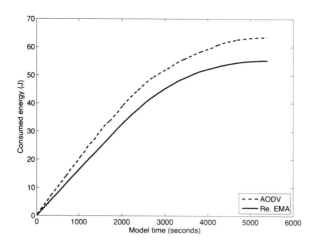

Figure 7.12: Energy consumption for AODV and Reactive EMA

When the energy consumption is put into relation to the transmission success rate, the energy per successfully transmitted data packet, which is displayed in

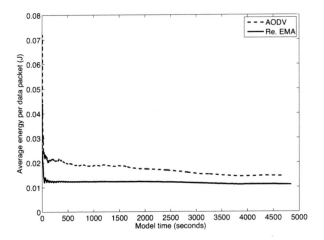

Figure 7.13: Energy spent in the network per successful transmission, for AODV and Reactive EMA

figure 7.13, shows the advantage of Reactive EMA even more clearly. The figure shows the development of the average value of the quotient $\frac{total \quad energy \quad consumed}{successful \quad transmissions}$ over the simulation duration. It can be seen that the energy spent per packet is higher for AODV than for Reactive EMA throughout the whole simulation.

Comparison to OLSR   As a proactive protocol, OLSR is used for comparison. As for AODV, the available Opnet model is used here on top of 802.15.4 lower layers. Also comparable to the settings used for AODV, messages that are sent regularly, in this case Hello messages are sent every 15 seconds and the more energy-consuming Topology Control messages are sent at intervals of 30 seconds.

As OLSR is not only regularly broadcasting Hello messages but also Topology Control messages, and those messages are forwarded in the network, it can be expected that OLSR consumes more energy. This expectation is proven by the results displayed in figure 7.14.

Interpreting the results concerning the successful data transmissions, which are shown in figure 7.15, and also comparing them to the AODV results shown in figure 7.10, it can be seen that OLSR delivers more data than AODV, but still, the Reactive EMA protocol outperforms both in these statistics. Similar to AODV, the signal strength is not used as a decision parameter in OLSR, so the protocol some-

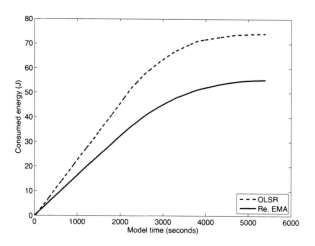

Figure 7.14: Energy consumption for OLSR and Reactive EMA

times selects routes with a low signal strength, which leads to more transmission failures.

The comparison to both OLSR and AODV, which are not context-aware, shows that context information such as signal strength can significantly improve the performance in aspects such as reliability.

Comparison to Proactive EMA   As a proactive context-aware protocol, the Proactive EMA [WPTGG08] is chosen for comparison. In both cases, the same route evaluation function is used, and the route lifetime is set to 30 seconds. To also maintain comparability to the AODV and OLSR results shown before, the regularly occurring transmissions (in this case: beacons) are done with an inter-beacon interval of 15 seconds. In proactive EMA, nodes are only forwarding the beacons if either a new best neighbour node was elected or the beacon refreshes the context information for an existing best neighbour. In this way, beacon floods are reduced to a required minimum. Especially if the network is static, this means that the only beacons being transmitted are those that refresh the best neighbour entries to avoid route expiry. Figure 7.16 reflects this in the energy consumption: The Proactive EMA consumes far less energy than the Reactive EMA. This does not contradict what was said in previous chapters about the comparison of proac-

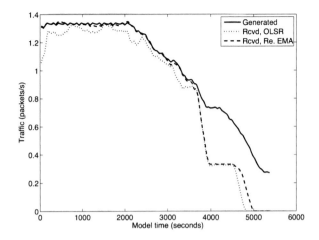

Figure 7.15: Data delivered at the sink, OLSR vs. Reactive EMA

tive and reactive routing, but the Proactive EMA here benefits from the network being quite static.

Unlike AODV and OLSR, the Proactive EMA achieves comparable success of data delivery as Reactive EMA. Both generally get their data to the sink as long as there is a way to reach it, as being shown in figure 7.17. This underlines the importance of context-awareness in the given scenario.

To sum up the findings from the comparison of the four protocols, it can be said that both EMA protocols outperform the others in terms of successful transmissions. The efficient beacon forwarding strategy of Proactive EMA makes it the most energy efficient protocol in this scenario, where the sensor nodes are immobile and the only source of dynamics is the fire which gradually kills the sensor nodes.

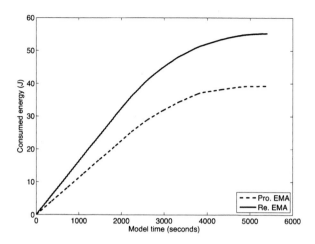

Figure 7.16: Energy consumption for Proactive and Reactive EMA

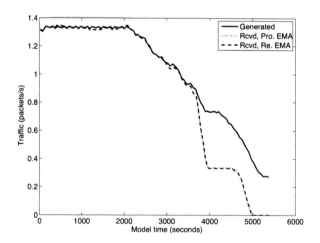

Figure 7.17: Data delivered at the sink, Proactive vs. Reactive EMA

7.4.2.3 Multiple Sinks

The design of the Reactive EMA protocol allows the use of multiple redundant sinks. Multiple sinks can increase the probability of data delivery, as there may still be a second or third sink which is reachable if the route to one sink cannot be used any more. The following simulation results show whether this theoretical advantage also can be proven in the simulation scenario. In the previously used scenario layout, a second sink is added at the upper right corner of the area, and a third one in the lower left corner.

Figure 7.18 shows the data delivery results for one, two and three sinks. As expected, each of both sinks improves the results. As after the addition of the third sink, the delivery rate reaches the generation rate also when a significant amount of nodes is destroyed, a fourth sink is not necessary here.

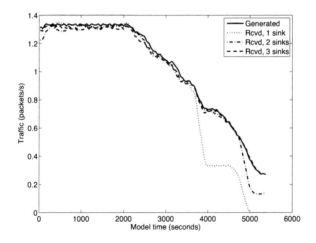

Figure 7.18: Successfully transmitted data in case of multiple sinks

When additional network nodes (either sensor nodes or sink nodes) are added to the network, more traffic and therefore more energy consumption is usually to be expected. Figure 7.19 shows that, in contrast to the expectation, the addition of the second and third sink cause a reduction of energy consumption. The explanation for this is that now, shorter routes to the sinks are possible, which reduces energy consumption during data transmission and overcompensates the increase in energy spent on the route discovery signalling.

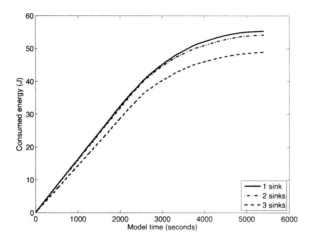

Figure 7.19: Energy consumption in case of multiple sinks

7.4.2.4 Reactive and Proactive EMA under Presence of Mobility

In a step towards a more dynamic evaluation scenario, sensor node mobility was introduced to the previous (single-sink) scenario. Mobile sensor nodes in a forest monitoring scenario may be, for example, animals that are carrying sensors. When real animals (not the sensors) become aware of a fire break out, of course, their movement patterns would be different from what is used here in the simulation, but this is not investigated in more detail here, instead, a standard mobility model is chosen.

The nodes in the scenario were configured to move according to a random direction mobility model [RMSM01] with speeds between 1 and 5 m/s, the speed distribution is uniform in that interval. The individual node movements now have two general influences on the results:

- depending on where they move, the fire reaches them sooner or later,
- also depending on the movement, routes to the sink are temporarily not available for some nodes.

This makes it necessary to run multiple simulation runs with different seeds so that different movement patterns are involved in the results. To ensure that the movement patterns for the simulations with Proactive and Reactive EMA are the same when the seed is the same, a separate random number generator was used for the mobility process. This generator is not a built-in generator of Opnet but an external generator that was taken from the CNCL library and included into the Opnet simulation following the example described in [BWLG07].

Figures 7.20 and 7.21 show exemplary results of the generated and delivered data, both for Reactive and for Proactive EMA. The difference between the settings of example 1 and example 2 is only the seed for the random number generators. This creates two different instances of the node mobility pattern. The figures prove both of the two points mentioned above: The curves for the generated traffic are different, so the different movement patterns must have lead to different times of node failure. Furthermore, in both cases, there were breakdowns in the amount of delivered traffic, followed by peaks that are above the generation rate. Here, the sink was temporarily unreachable for some of the nodes, and when they were able to establish a connection again, they flushed their buffers and sent out pending messages.

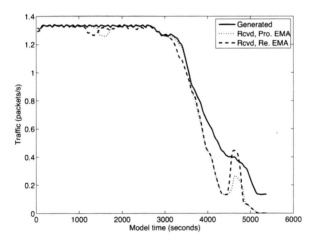

Figure 7.20: Generated and delivered traffic, example 1 for Proactive and Reactive EMA with node mobility

Especially from example 2 which is displayed in figure 7.21, it can be seen that Reactive EMA can recover faster when a significant portion of the sensor network was out of sink connectivity and regains the connectivity again. In Proactive EMA, the sensor nodes first have to reestablish their neighbour tables based on incoming

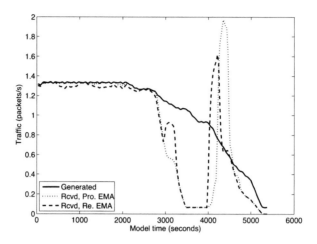

Figure 7.21: Generated and delivered traffic, example 2 for Proactive and Reactive EMA with node mobility

beacons, which temporarily generates significant beacon traffic and also leads to a high collision rate when a lot of sensors simultaneously try to send their buffered data.

As the total energy consumption in the network depends on the node movement as well, the results for the consumed energy are displayed as sets of curves in figure 7.22. The figure is based on 10 simulation runs for Reactive EMA and 10 runs for Proactive EMA. Despite the different simulation seeds, which created different movement patterns although the nodes' initial positions remain the same, the consumed energy curves for the protocols form two groups which are only slightly overlapping. Of those groups, the one for the Reactive EMA is the one with higher amount of consumed energy. Towards the end if the simulated time, the curve groups spread, which can be explained by the different mobility patterns causing different node failure times. The longer more nodes are active, the more energy is consumed in total. The two black curves correspond to the "example 2" which was already introduced in the traffic charts. Here, it can be seen that the Proactive EMA shows a steep increase in the energy consumption when the previously disconnected part of the sensor network regains connectivity. In the energy consumption of Reactive EMA, this phenomenon is also visible but not as significant as for the Proactive EMA. On the other hand, during the time when most of the network is disconnected from the sink, Proactive EMA does not consume much energy while the energy consumption of Reactive EMA increases due to repeated route discoveries.

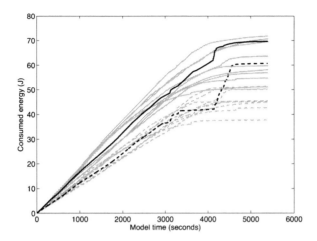

Figure 7.22: Energy consumption of Proactive (dashed) and Reactive (solid) EMA with node mobility. The black lines represent the energy consumption corresponding to the traffic shown in figure 7.21

In this mobility scenario, the Reactive EMA still consumes more energy than the Proactive EMA, which is an indication that the traffic caused by route discoveries in Reactive EMA is higher than the beacon traffic in Proactive EMA. With respect to scalability, more advanced flood limitation approaches will be required to ensure acceptable resource utilisation in networks with higher density.

7.5 Reactive and Proactive EMA with Sleep Cycles

The scenarios and simulation results shown up to here assume that all nodes are continuously online. But to extend node and network lifetime, sleep cycles are often considered to be a good way of energy optimisation (e.g. [SF06]). If individual sleep cycles of the nodes are assumed, the network topology becomes more dynamic and the routing protocols have to handle this.

Therefore, the simulations in the static network (i.e. without mobility) were repeated with sensor nodes that perform sleep cycles. In the investigated setup, the nodes were set to sleep 50% of their sensing cycle time, which means they are deactivated for 7.5 seconds within their 15 second sensing interval. They wake up 0.1 seconds before their scheduled sensing time, stay awake for 7.5 seconds, and go into sleep mode again afterwards. The sink remains active throughout the complete simulation time.

Figure 7.23 shows the generated and delivered traffic when Reactive EMA is used with the described sleep cycle settings. Compared to figure 7.6, it can be seen that now, the first node failures already have an impact on the amount of successful transmissions. As not all nodes are awake at the same time, there are obviously less route options, and the failures of individual nodes have a stronger impact.

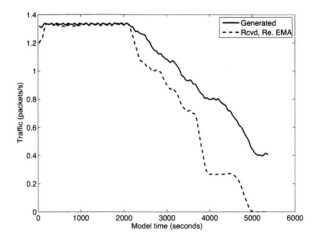

Figure 7.23: Generated and delivered traffic, Reactive EMA with 50% sleep time

The generated and delivered traffic for Proactive EMA is shown in figure 7.25. The left graph shows that, without any changes to the beacon interval, much of the generated traffic does not reach the sink. The reason is that, if the nodes are sleeping when the sink transmits the beacons, they miss the beacons and therefore do not get any information about the network. So if the Proactive EMA should work properly in a network where the nodes do sleep cycles, it either requires the awake periods to be synchronised to the beacons, or beacons have to be transmitted more frequently so that all nodes can receive some during their awake periods. For the right graph in figure 7.25, a beacon interval of 3 seconds was used in Proactive EMA. Still, the results show more successful transmissions for Reactive EMA. The corresponding energy consumption graphs are shown in figure 7.24. It can be seen that the increased beacon frequency causes the Proactive EMA to consume more energy than the Reactive EMA. When this figure is compared to figure 7.16, it can be stated that, because of the higher beacon frequency, the energy consumption in Proactive EMA is hardly reduced by the use of sleep cycles, while Reactive EMA consumes much less energy. With the use of sleep cycles, the performance of Reactive EMA becomes better than that of Proactive EMA.

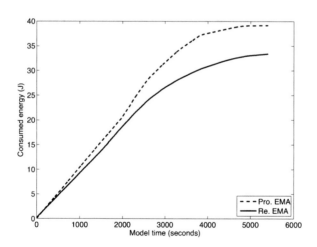

Figure 7.24: Energy consumption, Reactive and Proactive EMA with 50% sleep time

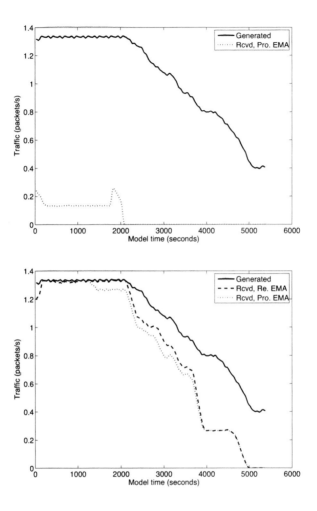

Figure 7.25: Generated and delivered traffic, Proactive EMA with 50% sleep time and beacon intervals of 15 seconds (upper figure) and 3 seconds (lower figure)

7.6 Summary of this Chapter

In this chapter, the Reactive EMA implementation and its simulation in OPNET has been presented in detail. Results of simulations with different settings were presented, as well as comparisons to simulations with other protocols. It was shown that Reactive EMA performs better than standard protocols such as AODV and OLSR. When sleep cycles are used on the nodes in the wireless sensor network, Reactive EMA has also shown advantages over its proactive counterpart. All in all, it can be said that Reactive EMA successfully applies the generic context-aware routing protocol to wireless sensor networks, and that the achieved results underline the advantages of context awareness for routing in wireless sensor networks.

For further performance improvements, Reactive EMA may be extended by a context aware power control component. Such an extension could further optimise the energy consumption in the network (and thereby the network lifetime) and the scalability in large or dense networks.

8 Conclusions and Outlook

In this thesis, a generalised context-aware routing concept was presented that can be used in different application domains. This routing concept includes the signalling as well as the route decision method. The routing traffic was analysed, and specialisations of the routing concept were shown for logistic networks and wireless sensor networks.

8.1 Conclusions

The general routing concept presented in chapter 3 of this thesis is a concept with reactive route discovery and context-based route decisions. Based on the specified signalling, the routing concept can be categorised into the family of source routing protocols. When a route is needed, the routing starts with a route discovery. Route discovery is done by flooding route request messages into the network, which trigger the generation of route replies at the traffic destination. This use of route request and route reply messages is similar to Dynamic Source Routing (DSR) [JM96] in mobile ad-hoc communication networks. The route choice is done at the source of the traffic after reception of several route reply messages.

Route request and route reply messages contain data fields for the context that is relevant for the routing. These data fields are also defined in this thesis, they contain a specification of the relevant context, advice on how this context is to be handled (i.e. scaling and evaluation rules) and of course the context values themselves.

Based on the general concept, specialised versions were designed for wireless sensor networks and logistic networks. In wireless sensor networks, the resulting protocol is the Reactive EMA routing. It extends the general message formats to the specific use in sensor networks, while the route discovery itself works as specified in the general protocol.

In logistic networks, the Distributed Logistic Routing Protocol (DLRP) is the specialised version. Here, the general design has to be extended as there are different entities (vehicles and goods) that simultaneously do route discoveries and have to match their routes in order to achieve efficient logistics. Therefore, route announcements and route disannouncements are added to the messaging scheme. Furthermore, due to the duration of transports, context changes occur while the transport is ongoing. This requires the ability to change routes during transport according to the changes of the context. Therefore, routes are re-evaluated by vehicles and goods during the transport process, which means there are usually several route discoveries during a transport.

For the context-based decision, the Multi-Criteria Context-based Decision function (MCCD) is proposed in chapter 4. This function combines multiple context parameters into one metric. The combination is done by a weighted multiplication of the context criteria. Each of the criteria is scaled into a common value range before the weighted multiplication is applied.

With respect to the amount of routing message traffic that is created by the proposed routing method, an analysis is conducted in chapter 5. This analysis shows that the traffic is a critical issue for scalability in large networks. Approaches to limit the forwarding of route requests are discussed as promising ways to reduce the traffic, but it is also pointed out that the characteristics of the context criteria being used have an influence on the efficiency of the limitation.

The DLRP routing with MCCD is evaluated by simulation in chapter 6. In this evaluation, a scenario with a topology based on a map of Germany is used, where goods have to be transported between the locations in this topology. It was shown that the achieved logistic performance can be improved in comparison to other routing approaches. Furthermore, the influences of weight variations for individual context criteria were shown, and it was shown that carefully chosen route request limitations can reduce the signalling volume while, at the same time, the logistic performance level can be maintained or even improved.

The simulative evaluation of Reactive EMA in wireless sensor networks is presented in chapter 7. The simulation results show that the context awareness leads to an improved data delivery reliability compared to non-context-aware protocols, while the energy consumption in the simulated scenario was also competitive. Additionally, Reactive EMA proved to work well in scenarios with multiple redundant sinks, and in scenarios with mobility.

So, in both the logistic and the sensor network scenarios, it was shown that the developed routing concept handles the required routing tasks in these scenarios well. The specialisations of the concept have shown good results in comparison to other routing approaches in the respective domains.

The routing traffic analysis as well as the simulations have shown that the amount of communication traffic that is generated by route discoveries is a critical issue towards scalability. It was shown that route request forwarding limitations are a reasonable way to reduce the traffic, but some effort has to be made to design a proper setup for efficient traffic reduction without causing too frequent route discovery failures.

8.2 Outlook

The volume of control traffic, especially during the route discovery, has shown to be a critical issue when operating a reactive context-aware routing protocol. Forwarding limitations for route request messages were applied in the simulations shown in this thesis, the limitation decisions were binary decisions, either a node forwards route requests, or it does not. To achieve a more efficient use of resources especially in dense or large-scale networks, a promising idea is to extend these decisions to a selective forwarding approach, i.e. it is not only decided whether to forward or not, but it could be decided to which of the neighbour nodes the request should be forwarded. This requires some knowledge about the network topology to elect proper forwarding targets. A way to obtain this required knowledge is using cached information from previous route discoveries.

Independent of whether the forwarding decisions are binary or selective, adaptive forwarding limits are possible enhancements. The adaptation can take the local network density or other criteria into account. This can be beneficial especially for wireless sensor networks, where channel congestion can be a problem in dense areas of the network. If less route requests are forwarded in those dense areas, the congestion will be reduced or even avoided.

In the logistic simulations, it could be noticed that goods originating from vertices at the borders of the scenario (e.g. Berlin or Munich in the simulated topologies) are much more probable to experience delays than those originating in the center. This is even more the case if both the origin and the destination are located at the border. In general, that is not surprising, as there are more routes going through centre vertices, so they are visited more often. Here, it would be useful to make the vehicles visit the border vertices more frequently. An additional context criterion for the vehicles' route choice can be designed to achieve this. This criterion needs to be a representation of the global optimisation goal of fair distribution of vehicle visits. For such a criterion, vertices have to compare their incoming amount of goods (either originated locally or carried by incoming vehicles) to the incoming transport capacity. If this relation is unbalanced, the vertices have to modify the respective criterion such that a more suitable amount of vehicles gets attracted.

Furthermore, the logistic scenarios should be extended towards additional realistic constraints, which means that the information on selected routes does not flow freely between all participating actors, but some vehicles or goods will probably decide to hold back some information due to security concerns or operator policies. Here, the DLRP requires extensions to represent levels of interaction and trust. Also, the current logistic model just considers vehicles and goods as entities that require routes. Here, a step further towards the real world applicability of the model and the DLRP would be to integrate containers and other units that usually contain a "bundle" of goods.

8.3 Final Statement

This thesis presents a context-based routing framework which can be realised in different application domains. The routing framework includes the signalling as well as a decision system that is applied for route selection. Through analytical and simulative evaluation, the routing framework is shown to be a good method for context-based routing in dynamic environments. This routing framework can be considered as a basis for future research in the area of context-based routing, as it opens manifold directions for further applications and enhancements.

Appendix

A Proactive Environmental Monitoring Aware Routing

The Proactive variant of Environmental Monitoring Aware routing, Proactive EMA, which was introduced in [WPTGG08], shows that EMA routing can also be done proactively. As this routing protocol is referred to in different sections of this thesis, it is described in this appendix chapter.

Proactive EMA is a sink-initiated proactive routing protocol. In contrast to Reactive EMA, it is not that flexible but bound to the predefined set of context parameters, which are the *node health*, the *RSSI* (Received Signal Strength Indicator) and the *hop count*.

A.1 Route Update Signalling

Routing table creation and maintenance in Proactive EMA is based on beacons that are transmitted in the network. Each sink in the network triggers route updates by sending out periodic beacons. These *sink beacons* contain information about the sink's health and a hop count of 0. The content of the RSSI field, which is also present in the beacons, is undefined for sink beacons. A sensor node which receives a sink beacon (identified by the hop count value) determines the RSSI for this beacon and updates an internal *sink table* with the new information, including the measured RSSI value. Then it modifies the beacon by increasing the hop count by 1 and setting the health value to the lower of its own health and the health value from the received beacon. In this way, the beacon message always contains the lowest health value on the route. Additionally, the RSSI value is added to the beacon so that a quality indication of the path is available for the next nodes. After these changes, the beacon is rebroadcast.

The rebroadcast beacons (*neighbour beacons*) are then received by other nodes, of which some may not be in direct communication range of the sink. Upon receipt of a neighbour beacon, a node compares the current information about health, RSSI and hop count to the information it already has about the sending neighbour node and updates its internal *neighbour table* accordingly. If it did not have any information on that neighbour node yet, it creates a new neighbour table entry. Then it elects its best neighbour node. If there is a change related to the best neighbour, the beacon is rebroadcast with updated health, RSSI and hop count information. A "change related to the best neighbour" means that one of the following conditions is fulfilled:

- a new best neighbour is elected,
- a new beacon was received from the current best neighbour.

If there is no change related to the elected best neighbour, the neighbour beacon is not rebroadcast to save energy and to reduce network load. The rebroadcasting of each beacon from the best neighbour has two reasons: integration of new nodes and avoidance of route expiry. Integration of new nodes means that new sensor nodes which are joining the network can easily be integrated as beacons occur regularly. A route expiry can occur because either the topology changes or nodes fail. To avoid that the failure of a best neighbour remains undiscovered, a timeout is defined after which a neighbour table entry becomes invalid. The timeout has to be longer than the beacon interval so that it only occurs if there are no periodic beacons from the best neighbour any more. In the case of a timeout, a new best neighbour is elected.

A.2 Best Neighbour Election

Each node sorts both its neighbour table and its sink table according to a multiplicative utility function that has basically the same form as the *Multi-Criteria Context-based Decision function* (MCCD) that is introduced in chapter 4 of this thesis, with the only difference that all weights are set to 1:

$$U = \prod_{i=1}^{k}(f_{s,i}(c_i))\tag{A.1}$$

where c_i is the value of the i-th context criterion and $f_{s,i}$ is a scaling function that maps c_i to the interval $[0,1]$. In the case of the neighbour table, the context criteria are the already mentioned criteria health, hop count and RSSI. For these criteria, the following settings were applied:

- **The health** is a parameter defined between 0 and 100. As good health is preferable, a linear downscaling, dividing by 100, can be used for this criterion.
- **The hop count** can be any non-negative integer value. As low hop counts are preferable, the scaling function should have its maximum for a hop count of 0 and be 0 for an infinite hop count. A negative exponential scaling function was chosen because it facilitates mapping of the possible hop count range $[0 \; \infty]$ onto the interval $[0 \; 1]$, with 0 hops being mapped onto 1.
- **The RSSI value** is given in dBW, and as long as the transmission power of the nodes is below 1 W (which is usually the case in wireless sensor networks), the RSSI always has a negative value. A high RSSI is preferable here. The scaling function chosen is a positive exponential function, which projects the value range $[-\infty \; 0]$ into the interval $[0 \; 1]$. The exponent here has to be adapted to the usual value range of the RSSI in order to avoid that the RSSI criterion dominates the other two criteria.

The complete metric used here is

$$U = \frac{health}{100} * e^{-hopcount} * e^{\frac{RSSI}{50}}.$$ (A.2)

For sorting of the sink table, the hop count is not used, as it is always the same for a direct link to a sink. The health and RSSI are used in the same manner as for the neighbour table.

The best neighbour selection then works as follows:

- **If sinks are in communication range**, the best sink is elected as best neighbour node, thus using direct communication to the sink whenever this is possible.
- **If no sink is in communication range**, a neighbour node has to act as a multi-hop relay towards the sink. In this case, the best node from the neighbour table is elected.

A.3 Sensor Data Transmission

Whenever a sensor node has data to send, communication to the sink takes place on a hop-by-hop basis. The sending node looks up the current best neighbour node in the neighbour table and forwards its data to that node. The receiving node then does the same, and in this way the data packets travel through the network until they reach the destination. Acknowledgements are also transmitted according to this hop-by-hop forwarding: there are no end-to-end acknowledgements, but instead there are acknowledgements on each hop. This is sufficient for most sensor network scenarios where end-to-end acknowledged transmissions are not required. If an application relies on end-to-end acknowledgements, e.g. to fulfil QoS requirements, there has to be an additional end-to-end acknowledgement support, which could be provided by only acknowledging a transmission if the subsequent hop has been acknowledged. In this case, however, acknowledgement timeouts have to be dimensioned according to the expected maximum hop count in the sensor network.

B Decision Concept in [SRRWM08]

As the decision concept that was used for the results presented in [SRRWM08] is used to generate results for comparison in subsection 6.4.2, this concept is sketched here. It is an empirically chosen decision concept based on experiences of earlier simulations.

B.1 Goods Routing

The goods routing is kept simple here, the only decision criterion is the route length. 3 alternative routes are announced, each with a preference that is based on the route length. To be exact, the preference of route i is defined as

$$Pref_i = \frac{(1/routelength_i)^3}{\sum_{j=1}^{3}(1/routelength_j)^3} \tag{B.1}$$

where j is the index that represents the announced routes.

B.2 Vehicle Routing

The vehicle routing is more complex than the goods routing. The optimisation goal is the vehicle utilisation here. Based on the existing route announcements at the vertices, an estimated amount of available load is calculated. This estimate consists of two parts: The estimated amount of goods and the estimated available transport capacity, both calculated individually for each route hop.

The estimated amount of goods takes all goods route announcements into account that are present for a specific next hop, not equally weighted but according to their announced preference and the number of hops in the announced route:

$$N_{Goods,est,hop\_i} = \sum \left(Size * Pref * \frac{1}{hops+1} \right). \tag{B.2}$$

It has to be noted that the term $\frac{1}{hops+1}$ stands for the probability that the piece of good is really at the vertex when the vehicle arrives. For goods that are already present, this term is removed.

The estimated available transport capacity is similarly calculated but with a probability of decision change instead of a preference:

$$N_{Vehcap,est,hop\_i} = \sum \left(Capacity * Changeprob * \frac{1}{hops+1} \right). \tag{B.3}$$

For vehicles already present at the vertex, only the capacity is taken into account.

The estimated available load is then the difference between the available goods and the available transport capacity:

$$N_{Load,est,hop\_i} = N_{Goods,est,hop\_i} - NVehcap, est, hop\_i \qquad (B.4)$$

The actual route decision is based on the available load on each route option, which is combined from the estimated available load at each of the hops. Additionally, routes that match those of goods which are currently on board and/or continue the current vehicle route get awarded a bonus. In this way, some stability of routes can be achieved. This is necessary because it was shown e.g. in [WPTG06] that too frequent route changes can lead to a reduced performance.

C Result Tables of Individual Logistic Simulation Runs

Table C.1: Individual results for table 6.3

Weight	Mean delay	Median delay	Capacity utilisation	Average rel. distance	Package cost (mu/km)	Delivered packages
1	10.6014	1.7010	0.7783	1.3560	2.0089	24295
	8.0834	2.1470	0.7882	1.3770	1.9261	24361
	7.2282	1.3500	0.7712	1.3468	1.9243	24553
	7.9003	1.8990	0.7715	1.3389	1.9426	24502
	7.8098	1.8680	0.7715	1.3358	1.9554	24434
	7.7280	1.9930	0.7626	1.3189	1.9016	24403
	8.4120	1.9890	0.7752	1.3346	1.9396	24445
	8.1054	1.5785	0.7654	1.3570	1.9923	24062
	7.3372	2.1500	0.7586	1.3173	1.8563	24557
	8.1436	2.3290	0.7673	1.3337	1.9077	24379
2	9.0160	1.8133	0.7762	1.3492	1.9693	24300
	8.1118	2.1700	0.7856	1.3608	1.9139	24331
	6.6724	1.5280	0.7563	1.3239	1.8976	24549
	7.9003	1.8990	0.7715	1.3389	1.9426	24502
	8.3628	2.0620	0.7749	1.3472	1.9804	24381
	7.6030	1.9188	0.7492	1.2926	1.9138	24403
	8.6341	2.0410	0.7751	1.3352	1.9439	24417
	8.1054	1.5785	0.7654	1.3570	1.9923	24062
	7.1060	2.1004	0.7612	1.3227	1.8600	24542
	8.1532	2.4000	0.7796	1.3824	2.0439	24403

Table C.1: Individual results for table 6.3 (continued)

Weight	Mean delay	Median delay	Capacity utilisation	Average rel. distance	Package cost (mu/km)	Delivered packages
3	8.8273	1.6855	0.7760	1.3476	1.9625	24346
	8.9522	2.3405	0.7878	1.3701	1.9461	24338
	6.6070	1.5420	0.7592	1.3258	1.9024	24567
	7.6515	1.7260	0.7703	1.3344	1.9370	24391
	8.3046	2.1028	0.7721	1.3459	1.9876	24334
	7.5806	1.9140	0.7485	1.2930	1.9102	24377
	8.7427	2.1220	0.7785	1.3500	1.9678	24357
	8.6607	1.7150	0.7627	1.3347	1.9992	24205
	7.1060	2.1004	0.7612	1.3227	1.8600	24542
	7.8393	2.1150	0.7642	1.3310	1.9567	24299
4	8.8273	1.6855	0.7760	1.3476	1.9625	24346
	8.7297	2.3890	0.7868	1.3663	1.9372	24388
	7.8010	1.5830	0.7816	1.3873	1.9818	24556
	7.4775	1.7780	0.7691	1.3357	1.9316	24321
	7.4032	1.9860	0.7693	1.3407	1.9340	24445
	7.5147	1.8190	0.7503	1.2909	1.9151	24426
	8.7452	2.1650	0.7748	1.3346	1.9639	24435
	8.6607	1.7150	0.7627	1.3347	1.9992	24205
	7.3254	2.0720	0.7604	1.3195	1.8767	24543
	8.2596	2.4110	0.7726	1.3764	2.0495	24225
5	9.6907	1.9480	0.7730	1.3631	2.0129	24042
	8.8520	2.5415	0.7907	1.3796	1.9263	24278
	7.8010	1.5830	0.7816	1.3873	1.9818	24556
	7.4775	1.7780	0.7691	1.3357	1.9316	24321
	7.4032	1.9860	0.7693	1.3407	1.9340	24445
	7.4828	1.8400	0.7498	1.2919	1.9191	24447
	8.7518	2.0630	0.7766	1.3405	1.9603	24427
	8.2193	1.7813	0.7592	1.3285	2.0009	24306
	7.1518	2.1417	0.7619	1.3254	1.8445	24604
	7.8632	2.4140	0.7678	1.3550	2.0284	24224

Table C.1: Individual results for table 6.3 (continued)

Weight	Mean delay	Median delay	Capacity utilisation	Average rel. distance	Package cost (mu/km)	Delivered packages
25	9.4460	2.0600	0.7785	1.3441	2.0287	24443
	8.7504	2.2060	0.7924	1.3649	1.9452	24277
	7.6015	1.4156	0.7721	1.3497	1.9364	24437
	7.4340	1.6380	0.7692	1.3321	1.9399	24504
	7.9481	2.0310	0.7713	1.3435	1.9708	24470
	7.4524	1.8660	0.7520	1.2957	1.9002	24490
	8.8122	2.0600	0.7828	1.3442	1.9774	24530
	8.1524	1.6230	0.7621	1.3304	2.0134	24256
	7.8510	2.3100	0.7593	1.3223	1.8804	24566
	7.9795	2.4685	0.7679	1.3758	1.9837	24328
100	9.4355	2.2480	0.7786	1.3541	2.0390	24237
	8.8468	2.5620	0.7999	1.3852	1.9354	24273
	7.5977	1.4290	0.7694	1.3079	1.9344	24600
	8.3772	1.9390	0.7649	1.3283	1.9635	24335
	7.3644	2.0230	0.7757	1.3480	1.9459	24359
	7.9468	1.9634	0.7538	1.2936	1.9125	24459
	8.0011	1.9290	0.7704	1.3106	1.9154	24525
	8.7539	1.8505	0.7615	1.3389	2.0123	24332
	8.0037	2.3400	0.7647	1.3329	1.9070	24467
	8.1168	2.4070	0.7714	1.3717	2.0281	24305
500	8.9619	2.0370	0.7814	1.3512	1.9870	24394
	8.4647	2.1200	0.7990	1.3924	1.9310	24287
	6.8431	1.0450	0.7617	1.3212	1.9195	24635
	8.5825	2.1010	0.7721	1.3481	1.9775	24457
	7.8294	2.0039	0.7719	1.3460	1.9817	24310
	8.0265	2.0115	0.7672	1.3301	1.9241	24404
	8.5219	2.4395	0.7809	1.3396	1.9113	24384
	8.5587	1.8510	0.7603	1.3354	2.0468	24311
	7.3733	2.5270	0.7572	1.3062	1.8509	24561
	8.2077	2.6180	0.7685	1.3722	1.9995	24372

Table C.2: Individual results for table 6.4

Weight	Mean delay	Median delay	Capacity utilisation	Average rel. distance	Package cost (mu/km)	Delivered packages
1;2	10.6014	1.7010	0.7783	1.3560	2.0089	24295
5;25	8.0834	2.1470	0.7882	1.3770	1.9261	24361
	7.2282	1.3500	0.7712	1.3468	1.9243	24553
	7.9003	1.8990	0.7715	1.3389	1.9426	24502
	7.8098	1.8680	0.7715	1.3358	1.9554	24434
	7.7280	1.9930	0.7626	1.3189	1.9016	24403
	8.4120	1.9890	0.7752	1.3346	1.9396	24445
	8.1054	1.5785	0.7654	1.3570	1.9923	24062
	7.3372	2.1500	0.7586	1.3173	1.8563	24557
	8.1436	2.3290	0.7673	1.3337	1.9077	24379
100	9.4319	2.0330	0.7787	1.3625	2.0372	24184
	9.6351	1.8155	0.7777	1.3386	1.9966	24166
	6.5328	1.2537	0.7623	1.3371	1.9643	24570
	7.8994	1.4680	0.7856	1.3712	2.0413	24199
	8.2318	1.7941	0.7740	1.3555	2.0271	24485
	7.1045	1.7160	0.7616	1.3216	1.9002	24419
	9.1974	1.7830	0.7651	1.3029	1.9482	24490
	7.2729	1.5480	0.7509	1.3145	1.9367	24373
	7.4994	1.8930	0.7481	1.3080	1.8650	24525
	8.0458	2.2291	0.7616	1.3320	1.9748	24339
250	9.0565	1.0425	0.7740	1.3676	2.0184	23866
	8.6641	1.7235	0.7693	1.3533	2.0146	24244
	7.3432	1.8610	0.7669	1.3396	1.9688	24403
	8.5463	1.7230	0.7723	1.3498	1.9922	24351
	7.8118	1.9830	0.7717	1.3515	1.9830	24470
	8.5205	2.0760	0.7736	1.3753	1.9961	24385
	7.3279	1.2635	0.7592	1.3033	1.9259	24384
	7.8774	1.5005	0.7605	1.3557	1.9788	24332
	6.8629	2.0160	0.7459	1.2853	1.8446	24566
	7.7085	1.8655	0.7733	1.3887	2.0150	24460

Table C.2: Individual results for table 6.4 (continued)

Weight	Mean delay	Median delay	Capacity utilisation	Average rel. distance	Package cost (mu/km)	Delivered packages
500	6.6073	0.6990	0.7672	1.3221	1.9324	24533
	7.1922	1.1811	0.7674	1.3466	1.9479	24430
	5.8123	0.6830	0.7327	1.2917	1.9076	24548
	7.0233	0.8923	0.7522	1.3397	1.9484	24508
	5.7242	0.4000	0.7571	1.3055	1.9348	24491
	6.7343	0.2896	0.7582	1.3098	1.9685	24516
	5.9372	1.0400	0.7246	1.2594	1.8677	24547
	6.3242	0.6500	0.7383	1.2881	1.8998	24555
	6.3220	0.7074	0.7328	1.2445	1.8443	24558
	8.0423	1.1990	0.7553	1.3203	1.9644	24393
750	5.2081	-0.2080	0.7274	1.2666	1.8882	24073
	4.5215	-0.6640	0.7103	1.2451	1.8643	24114
	4.7809	0.1380	0.7083	1.2277	1.8636	24272
	4.7932	0.0595	0.7092	1.2315	1.8182	24226
	4.8385	0.3640	0.7217	1.2474	1.8324	24291
	5.1932	0.4575	0.7313	1.2645	1.8515	24290
	5.0387	0.2900	0.7342	1.2815	1.8419	24098
	5.6845	0.7320	0.7209	1.2502	1.8419	24182
	5.8318	0.7285	0.7296	1.2576	1.8514	24298
	5.1914	0.2190	0.7353	1.2742	1.8704	24163
990	3.7463	0.0700	0.7157	1.2058	1.7693	23745
	4.8096	0.6100	0.7030	1.2019	1.8190	23296
	3.7971	0.0655	0.6807	1.1745	1.7626	23580
	4.0800	-0.1335	0.6916	1.1792	1.7654	23710
	3.4730	-0.0020	0.7169	1.2256	1.7386	23451
	4.2303	0.2770	0.7034	1.2069	1.7618	23679
	4.9957	0.7030	0.7159	1.2559	1.8382	22940
	4.1974	0.2230	0.7023	1.2225	1.7936	23409
	3.4144	-0.2720	0.6814	1.1656	1.7180	23687
	4.7546	0.3595	0.6920	1.2016	1.7878	23084

Table C.3: Individual results for table 6.5

Weight	Mean delay	Median delay	Capacity utilisation	Average rel. distance	Package cost (mu/km)	Delivered packages
1	-1.1157	-7.7860	0.7827	1.3499	1.8568	23955
	-1.6573	-6.9790	0.7732	1.3312	1.7852	24201
	-0.6032	-6.3400	0.7929	1.3801	1.8503	24261
	-1.0526	-6.9630	0.7758	1.3483	1.8755	24014
	-2.2351	-6.8000	0.7779	1.3368	1.7883	24491
	-1.1887	-7.0450	0.8010	1.3821	1.8570	24379
	-1.1634	-6.8960	0.7751	1.3317	1.8066	24411
	-1.0991	-6.5787	0.7821	1.3645	1.8564	24366
	-1.3523	-6.3230	0.7783	1.3317	1.7834	24468
	-0.0405	-6.2150	0.7969	1.3825	1.8505	24321
2	0.2911	-7.8740	0.7786	1.3466	1.8732	23738
	-1.1846	-7.1870	0.7767	1.3445	1.8099	24211
	-0.3389	-6.4930	0.7939	1.3762	1.8637	24277
	-0.7472	-6.7983	0.7784	1.3370	1.8702	24264
	-2.2836	-6.8470	0.7823	1.3437	1.8029	24518
	-1.2101	-7.1000	0.7996	1.3831	1.8454	24379
	-0.7111	-6.9120	0.7774	1.3400	1.8215	24333
	-1.0991	-6.5787	0.7821	1.3645	1.8564	24366
	-0.6693	-6.2720	0.7777	1.3321	1.7988	24537
	-1.2042	-6.2844	0.7895	1.3648	1.7938	24456
3	-0.0370	-7.7860	0.7786	1.3461	1.8765	23821
	-0.4095	-6.8192	0.7749	1.3385	1.8145	23956
	-0.6774	-6.7410	0.7743	1.3462	1.8219	24278
	-0.7091	-6.9140	0.7773	1.3443	1.8761	24122
	-2.4212	-6.8420	0.7833	1.3448	1.8014	24513
	-1.2554	-6.7010	0.7937	1.3783	1.8025	24215
	-0.4918	-6.9510	0.7727	1.3383	1.8219	24106
	-1.0333	-6.7332	0.7791	1.3641	1.8408	24342
	-1.0751	-6.3155	0.7832	1.3329	1.7901	24508
	-1.0753	-6.4560	0.7851	1.3664	1.7965	24205

Table C.3: Individual results for table 6.5 (continued)

Weight	Mean delay	Median delay	Capacity utilisation	Average rel. distance	Package cost (mu/km)	Delivered packages
4	0.0287	-7.8800	0.7791	1.3447	1.8779	23848
	-1.0871	-7.0100	0.7749	1.3436	1.8192	24135
	-0.6774	-6.7410	0.7743	1.3462	1.8218	24278
	-0.7091	-6.9140	0.7773	1.3443	1.8761	24122
	-2.0633	-6.9980	0.7779	1.3336	1.8066	24463
	-0.6842	-6.6280	0.7949	1.3710	1.8537	24334
	-0.7613	-6.5305	0.7811	1.3328	1.8061	24410
	-1.5025	-6.6885	0.7827	1.3666	1.8406	24432
	-1.8268	-6.3990	0.7718	1.3058	1.7353	24511
	-1.0676	-6.3020	0.7867	1.3556	1.7870	24373
5	-1.2761	-7.3345	0.7688	1.3129	1.8117	24042
	-1.3143	-7.2331	0.7799	1.3363	1.8022	24223
	-1.4914	-6.8660	0.7757	1.3411	1.8018	24480
	-0.3867	-7.1300	0.7729	1.3298	1.8915	24144
	-1.8256	-6.8360	0.7785	1.3339	1.8156	24532
	-1.3968	-6.8835	0.7935	1.3571	1.8047	24342
	-0.7613	-6.5305	0.7811	1.3328	1.8061	24410
	-1.5025	-6.6885	0.7827	1.3666	1.8406	24432
	-1.0257	-6.3130	0.7754	1.3032	1.7759	24521
	-1.3264	-6.3077	0.7872	1.3604	1.7829	24477
25	0.2853	-7.4380	0.7811	1.3290	1.9021	24179
	-1.0632	-6.9590	0.7745	1.3351	1.7907	24177
	-1.7087	-6.6035	0.7667	1.3256	1.8024	24516
	-0.7505	-7.0430	0.7806	1.3517	1.8709	24237
	-2.2159	-6.9970	0.7838	1.3464	1.7943	24517
	-1.8920	-6.9010	0.7958	1.3658	1.7938	24326
	-0.2610	-7.0300	0.7675	1.3401	1.8275	23885
	-1.1537	-6.7650	0.7760	1.3465	1.8519	24339
	-1.3768	-6.5110	0.7646	1.3013	1.7693	24534
	-0.9851	-6.4140	0.7900	1.3663	1.8236	24359

Table C.3: Individual results for table 6.5 (continued)

Weight	Mean delay	Median delay	Capacity utilisation	Average rel. distance	Package cost (mu/km)	Delivered packages
100	-1.1157	-7.4040	0.7720	1.3155	1.8170	24383
	-1.4068	-7.0090	0.7802	1.3387	1.7831	24139
	-0.9622	-6.5180	0.7845	1.3500	1.8257	24476
	-1.7396	-7.2810	0.7772	1.3402	1.8011	24519
	-1.9345	-6.7660	0.7777	1.3321	1.7964	24413
	-0.9634	-6.6180	0.7942	1.3661	1.8160	24346
	-0.1940	-6.8885	0.7759	1.3387	1.8580	24068
	-1.3251	-6.7310	0.7758	1.3515	1.8289	24388
	-1.3529	-6.2030	0.7738	1.3125	1.7778	24513
	-1.6428	-6.4650	0.7854	1.3628	1.7990	24427
500	-1.7010	-7.4800	0.7692	1.3112	1.7966	24411
	-1.0356	-6.6365	0.7842	1.3501	1.8043	24290
	-0.7587	-6.2610	0.7905	1.3694	1.8282	24399
	-1.3876	-7.1653	0.7730	1.3369	1.8003	24427
	-1.0632	-6.3330	0.7893	1.3561	1.8481	24441
	-0.8615	-6.6910	0.7942	1.3720	1.8411	24304
	-0.8907	-6.9340	0.7680	1.3458	1.8260	23801
	-1.1625	-6.6520	0.7792	1.3620	1.8657	24362
	-1.7955	-6.5780	0.7614	1.2989	1.7792	24443
	-1.6354	-6.3400	0.7815	1.3533	1.7707	24443

Table C.4: Individual results for table 6.6

Weight	Mean delay	Median delay	Capacity utilisation	Average rel. distance	Package cost (mu/km)	Delivered packages
1;25	-1.1157	-7.7860	0.7827	1.3499	1.8568	23955
	-1.6573	-6.9790	0.7732	1.3312	1.7852	24201
	-0.6032	-6.3400	0.7929	1.3801	1.8503	24261
	-1.0526	-6.9630	0.7758	1.3483	1.8755	24014
	-2.2351	-6.8000	0.7779	1.3368	1.7883	24491
	-1.1887	-7.0450	0.8010	1.3821	1.8570	24379
	-1.1634	-6.8960	0.7751	1.3317	1.8066	24411
	-1.0991	-6.5787	0.7821	1.3645	1.8564	24366
	-1.3523	-6.3230	0.7783	1.3317	1.7834	24468
	-0.0405	-6.2150	0.7969	1.3825	1.8505	24321
100	-1.2737	-7.2600	0.7723	1.3160	1.8066	24289
	-0.3070	-6.1635	0.7988	1.3713	1.8361	24124
	-0.7894	-6.5160	0.7801	1.3395	1.8273	24219
	0.6521	-6.9181	0.7907	1.4126	1.8811	23730
	-1.1228	-6.6110	0.7930	1.3729	1.8500	24315
	-0.9525	-6.5550	0.7814	1.3440	1.8288	24443
	-0.1079	-7.0070	0.7629	1.3043	1.8194	24420
	-1.4633	-6.6070	0.7899	1.3782	1.8128	24478
	-1.5662	-6.4355	0.7761	1.3265	1.7849	24542
	-0.6106	-6.4100	0.7917	1.3608	1.8077	24318
250	0.2101	-7.1975	0.7963	1.3456	1.8246	24566
	-1.8802	-6.6130	0.7796	1.3521	1.7608	24440
	-1.8637	-6.4064	0.7671	1.3232	1.7702	24579
	-2.3731	-6.9780	0.7796	1.3237	1.7637	24471
	-1.7875	-6.9815	0.7742	1.3398	1.8176	24412
	-0.4803	-6.6655	0.8039	1.4254	1.8865	24264
	-1.0400	-7.1950	0.7763	1.3386	1.8436	24375
	-1.3857	-6.7460	0.7874	1.3631	1.7800	24459
	-1.8376	-6.7505	0.7617	1.3050	1.7618	24570
	-2.2345	-6.7620	0.7739	1.3370	1.7562	24449

Table C.4: Individual results for table 6.6 (continued)

Weight	Mean delay	Median delay	Capacity utilisation	Average rel. distance	Package cost (mu/km)	Delivered packages
500	-2.2650	-8.1034	0.7664	1.3527	1.7737	24444
	-2.8104	-7.9840	0.7557	1.3228	1.7504	24285
	-3.5458	-8.4535	0.7455	1.3024	1.7242	24566
	-2.3261	-7.9620	0.7810	1.3675	1.7878	24417
	-3.6854	-8.2160	0.7613	1.3122	1.7224	24423
	-2.3348	-8.2450	0.7812	1.3642	1.7935	24234
	-3.3466	-7.9710	0.7619	1.3228	1.7019	24483
	-4.0400	-8.0370	0.7408	1.2707	1.6704	24577
	-4.0666	-8.0790	0.7426	1.2635	1.6802	24577
	-3.8489	-7.9970	0.7558	1.3092	1.7031	24453
750	-4.8547	-8.5950	0.7433	1.2782	1.6319	24315
	-4.9815	-9.0135	0.7465	1.2913	1.6060	24174
	-5.6148	-9.0230	0.7114	1.2318	1.5868	24335
	-5.0643	-9.1810	0.7358	1.2740	1.6331	24299
	-4.8171	-8.8480	0.7346	1.2520	1.6303	24311
	-4.4278	-8.4165	0.7479	1.2978	1.6419	24292
	-4.9647	-8.6500	0.7386	1.2808	1.5903	24226
	-4.7361	-8.6950	0.7303	1.2671	1.6281	24191
	-4.3936	-8.6200	0.7322	1.2609	1.6244	24184
	-5.0229	-8.5900	0.7282	1.2543	1.6218	24258
1000	-6.3904	-9.2320	0.7153	1.1991	1.5224	23759
	-6.1789	-9.0970	0.6978	1.1756	1.5117	23707
	-6.9739	-9.6028	0.6982	1.2023	1.4754	23790
	-6.4172	-9.6210	0.6918	1.1788	1.4683	23767
	-6.2289	-9.1920	0.7076	1.2132	1.4759	23461
	-6.1968	-9.2305	0.6837	1.1688	1.4641	23538
	-6.0829	-9.0990	0.7114	1.2138	1.4981	23668
	-6.5907	-9.7840	0.6823	1.1822	1.4627	23397
	-6.4290	-9.4060	0.6907	1.1779	1.4738	23712
	-6.3395	-8.9320	0.7090	1.2312	1.4919	23244

Table C.4: Individual results for table 6.6 (continued)

Weight	Mean delay	Median delay	Capacity utilisation	Average rel. distance	Package cost (mu/km)	Delivered packages
1500	-8.5337	-10.2950	0.5551	1.1200	1.2339	18879
	-8.5768	-10.4080	0.5560	1.1243	1.2595	19155
	-8.0569	-9.9700	0.5592	1.1458	1.3017	18296
	-8.7568	-10.5720	0.5499	1.0955	1.2398	19403
	-7.9390	-9.8620	0.5499	1.1060	1.2950	18990
	-8.0398	-9.9485	0.5729	1.1225	1.2731	19646
	-8.7544	-10.4280	0.5594	1.1040	1.2658	19343
	-8.6601	-10.3595	0.5534	1.1287	1.2468	18950
	-8.5793	-10.3829	0.5612	1.1304	1.2747	19088
	-8.4109	-9.9170	0.5663	1.1184	1.2731	19369

D DLRP Message Sizes

Although the actual sizes of DLRP messages are dependent on implementation details and decisions about how detailed the carried information should be, rough estimations are done here to be able to discuss traffic volumes that are created by DLRP. The estimations are based on the minimal set of information that needs to be included. Furthermore, the following assumptions are made:

- addresses of logistic entities are 32-bit integers
- MCCD is used for the route decisions
- 3 context criteria are used in the decisions
- 3 scaling parameters are required per scaling function

Because of these assumptions, the calculated message sizes have to be regarded as examples. If more criteria or more complex scalings are used, the messages can grow larger.

D.1 Route Request Messages

In 3.3.3.1, it was already mentioned what the DLRP messages need to contain. This is now listed here in detail with sizes that are likely for the fields.

- vehicle/package flag (boolean, 1 bit)
- message type (2 bits)
- sender address (integer, 32 bit)
- destination address (integer, 32 bit)
- sequence number (short integer, 8 bit)
- time to live (short integer, 8 bit)
- due time (integer timestamp, 32 bit)
- size or capacity (floating point, 32 bit)
- hop list with multiple elements that consist of

    - hop address (integer, 32 bit)
    - expected arrival time (integer timestamp, 32 bit)
    - expected leave time (integer timestamp, 32 bit)

- context field with the following contents

    - context criteria identifier (3x 8 bit → 24 bit)
    - scaling type identifiers (3x 8 bit → 24 bit)

- scaling parameters (9x floating point, 32 bit → 288 bit)
- context weights (3x floating point, 32 bit → 96 bit)
- context limits (4x floating point, 32 bit → 128 bit)
- context values (3x floating point, 32 bit → 96 bit)

When these numbers are summed up, the resulting message size is $803 + n * 96$ bit, where n is the number of hops. Padding can be applied to create complete octets. Including the padding, the message size is $101 + n * 12$ Byte. Of course, this is the size at application level, and lower layer protocol (e.g. TCP/IP) overhead is not included.

D.2 Route Reply Messages

In implementations where the destination just copies the route request to a route reply, the message size remains the same, only the content of the message type field is changed, the time to live field is replaced by a hop count field and source and destination may be swapped. However, it can be assumed that the vehicle or package remembers with which parameters it has initiated the route discovery, so that the context field may be significantly reduced. If the route reply is cut down to the absolutely necessary information, the following contents remain:

- message type (2 bits)
- sender address (integer, 32 bit)
- destination address (integer, 32 bit)
- sequence number (short integer, 8 bit)
- hop count (short integer, 8 bit)
- hop list with multiple elements that consist of

    - hop address (integer, 32 bit)
    - expected arrival time (integer timestamp, 32 bit)
    - expected leave time (integer timestamp, 32 bit)

- context field with the following contents

    - context values (3x floating point, 32 bit → 96 bit)

In this case, the resulting message size is $178 + n * 96$ bit, or (with padding) $23 + n * 12$ Byte.

D.3 Route Announcement Messages

The route announcements inform a vertex about the planned arrival and departure of a vehicle or packet. For this, it has to contain at least the following fields:

- vehicle/package flag (boolean, 1 bit)
- message type (2 bits)
- sender address (integer, 32 bit)
- announcement number (short integer, 8 bit)
- expected arrival time (integer timestamp, 32 bit)
- expected leave time (integer timestamp, 32 bit)
- next hop address (integer, 32 bit)
- size or capacity (floating point, 32 bit)
- route preference (floating point, 32 bit)

The sum of these fields results in 203 bit, which, assuming the use of padding, corresponds to 26 Byte.

D.4 Route Disannouncement Messages

A route disannouncement needs to refer to a previous announcement, so it has to contain enough data to uniquely identify the announcement that has to be cancelled.

- vehicle/package flag (boolean, 1 bit)
- message type (2 bits)
- sender address (integer, 32 bit)
- announcement number (short integer, 8 bit)
- next hop address (integer, 32 bit)

This results in 75 bit, if padding is used to have complete octets, the disannouncement size is 10 Byte.

Bibliography

[AKK04]   J.N. Al-Karaki and A.E. Kamal. Routing techniques in wireless sensor networks: a survey. *IEEE Wireless Communications*, 11(6):6–28, December 2004.

[BB04]   J. Berger and M. Barkaoui. A parallel hybrid genetic algorithm for the vehicle routing problem with time windows. *Computers & Operations Research*, 31(12):2037–2053, October 2004.

[BC03]   S. Bandyopadhyay and E.J. Coyle. An energy efficient hierarchical clustering algorithm for wireless sensor networks. In *Proc. 22nd Annual Joint Conference of the IEEE Computer and Communications Societies (INFOCOM)*, volume 2, pages 1713–1723, April 2003.

[Bec04]   D. Beckett. Rdf/xml syntax specification (revised). W3C Recommendation (http://www.w3.org/TR/rdf-syntax-grammar/), February 2004.

[BWG05]   M. Becker, B.-L. Wenning, and C. Görg. Integrated simulation of communication networks and logistical networks - using object-oriented programming language features to enhance modelling. In A.N. Ince and E. Topuz, editors, *Modeling and Simulation Tools for Emerging Telecommunication Networks: Needs, Trends, Challenges and Solutions*, pages 279–287. Springer, 2005.

[BWG+06]   M. Becker, B.-L. Wenning, C. Görg, J.D. Gehrke, M. Lorenz, and O. Herzog. Agent-based and discrete event simulation of autonomous logistic process. In W. Borutzky, A. Orsoni, and R. Zobel, editors, *Proc. 20th European Conference on Modelling and Simulation*, pages 566–571, May 2006.

[BWLG07]   M. Becker, T.L. Weerawardane, X. Li, and C. Görg. Extending opnet modeler with external pseudo random number generators and statistical evaluation by the limited relative error algorithm. In N. Ince and A. Bragg, editors, *Recent Advances in Modeling and Simulation Tools for Communication Networks and Services*, pages 241–255. Springer, 2007.

[Cis00]   *Internetworking Technology Handbook*, chapter 39. Cisco Press, 3rd edition, 2000.

[CJ03]   T. Clausen and P. Jacquet. Optimized link state routing protocol (olsr). IETF RFC 3626, October 2003.

[Com08]   Communication Networks, University of Bremen. *CNCL Documentation*, 2008. http://www.comnets.uni-bremen.de/docs/cncl/index.html.

[Com09]   Communication Networks, University of Bremen. *LoCoSim Documentation*, 2009. http://www.comnets.uni-bremen.de/docs/locosim/index.html.

[CP07]   I. Chakeres and C. Perkins. Dynamic manet on-demand (dymo) routing. IETF draft: draft-ietf-manet-dymo-08, March 2007.

[DA99]   A.K. Dey and G.D. Abowd. Towards a better understanding of context and context-awareness. In *1st International Symposium on Handheld and Ubiquitous Computing (HUC)*, pages 304–307, June 1999.

[Dij59]   E.W. Dijkstra. A note on two problems in connexion with graphs. *Numerische Mathematik*, 1(1):269–271, December 1959.

[DR59]   G.B. Dantzig and J.H. Ramser. The truck dispatching problem. *Management Science*, 6(1):80–91, October 1959.

[Haa97]   Z.J. Haas. A new routing protocol for the reconfigurable wireless networks. In *Proc. 6th IEEE International Conference on Universal Personal Communications, IEEE ICUPC'97*, volume 2, pages 562–566, October 1997.

[HCB00]   W.R. Heinzelman, A. Chandrakasan, and H. Balakrishnan. Energy-efficient communication protocol for wireless microsensor networks. In *Proc. 33rd Annual Hawaii International Conference onSystem Sciences*, volume 2, pages 1–10, January 2000.

[HH06]   T.T. Huynh and C.S. Hong. An energy*delay efficient multi-hop routing scheme for wireless sensor networks. *IEICE Transactions on Inf. & Syst.*, E89-D(5):1654–1661, May 2006.

[HKB99]   W.R. Heinzelman, J. Kulik, and H. Balakrishnan. Adaptive protocols for information dissemination in wireless sensor networks. In *Proc. 5th annual International Conference on Mobile Computing and Networking(MOBICOM)*, pages 174–185, 1999.

[IEE03]   IEEE. *IEEE Standard for Information technology – Telecommunications and information exchange between systems – Local and metropolitan area networks – Specific requirements – Part 15.4: Wireless Medium Access Control (MAC) and Physical Layer (PHY) Specifications for Low-Rate Wireless Personal Area Networks (WPANs)*, 2003. Revised 2006.

[IGE00]   C. Intanagonwiwat, R. Govindan, and D. Estrin. Directed diffusion: a scalable and robust communication paradigm for sensor networks. In *Proc. 6th annual International Conference on Mobile Computing and Networking (MOBICOM)*, pages 56–67, 2000.

[Jaf84]   J.M. Jaffe. Algorithms for finding paths with multiple constraints. *Networks*, 14(1):95–116, 1984.

[JM96]   D. Johnson and D. Maltz. Dynamic source routing in ad hoc wireless networks. In T. Imielinski and H. Korth, editors, *Mobile Computing*, pages 153–181. 1996.

[KHB02]   J. Kulik, W.R. Heinzelman, and H. Balakrishnan. Negotiation-based protocols for disseminating information in wireless sensor networks. *Wireless Networks*, 8:169–185, 2002.

[LBA⁺05] Q. Li, J. Beaver, A. Amer, P.K. Chrysanthis, A. Labrinidis, and G. Santhankrishnan. Multi-criteria routing in wireless sensor-based pervasive environments. *Journal of Pervasive Computing and Communications*, 1(4):313–326, December 2005.

[LR02]   S. Lindsey and C.S. Raghavendra. Pegasis: Power efficient gathering in sensor information systems. In *Proc. IEEE Aerospace Conference*, volume 3, pages 3–1125 – 3–1130, March 2002.

[LR05]   Q. Liang and Q. Ren. Energy and mobility aware geographical multipath routing for wireless sensor networks. In *Proc. IEEE Wireless Communications and Networking Conference 2005*, pages 1867–1871, March 2005.

[Luk07]   A. Lukosius. Opportunistic routing in multi-sink mobile ad hoc wireless sensor networks. Master's thesis, Communication Networks, University of Bremen, 2007.

[MA01]   A. Manjeshwar and D.P. Agrawal. Teen: a routing protocol for enhanced efficiency in wireless sensor networks. In *Proc. 15th International Parallel and Distributed Processing Symposium*, pages 2009–2015, April 2001.

[MA02]   A. Manjeshwar and D.P. Agrawal. Apteen: a hybrid protocol for efficient routing and comprehensive information retrieval in wireless sensor networks. In *Proc. International Parallel and Distributed Processing Symposium 2002*, pages 195–202, April 2002.

[Mal98]   G. Malkin. Rip version 2. IETF RFC 2453, November 1998.

[McC87]   J. McCarthy. Generality in artificial intelligence. *Communications of the ACM*, 30(12):1030–1035, December 1987.

[McC93]   J. McCarthy. Notes on formalizing context. In *Proc. 13th International Joint Conference on Artificial Intelligence*, pages 555–560, 1993.

[MHM05]   M. Musolesi, S. Hailes, and C. Mascolo. Adaptive routing for intermittently connected mobile ad hoc networks. In *Proc. 6th IEEE International Symposium on a World of Wireless Mobile and Multimedia Networks (WoWMoM) 2005*, pages 183–189, 2005.

[MM98]   S. Mitrovic-Minic. Pickup and delivery problems: A survey. Technical report, Simon Fraser University, May 1998.

[MM06]   C. Mascolo and M. Musolesi. Scar: Context-aware adaptive routing in delay tolerant mobile sensor networks. In *Proc. 2006 International Conference on Wireless Communications and Mobile Computing*, pages 533–538, 2006.

[Moy98]   J. Moy. Ospf version 2. IETF RFC 2328, April 1998.

[MTT⁺06]   B. Malakooti, I. Thomas, S.K. Tanguturi, S. Gajurel, H. Kim, and K. Bhasin. Multiple criteria network routing with simulation results. In *Proc. 15th Industrial Engineering Research Conference (IERC)*, May 2006.

[MvH04]   D.L. McGuinness and F. van Harmelen. Owl ontology web language overview. W3C Recommendation (http://www.w3.org/TR/owl.features/), February 2004.

[Nat98]   United Nations. Kyoto protocol to the united nations framework convention on climate change. http://unfccc.int/resource/docs/convkp/kpeng.pdf, 1998.

[NB00]   W.P. Nanry and J.W. Barnes. Solving the pickup and delivery problem with time windows using reactive tabu search. *Transportation Research Part B*, 34(2):107–121, February 2000.

[OPN08]   OPNET. Opnet modeler. Web page: http://opnet.com/solutions/network_rd /modeler.html, 2008.

[otEC04]   Commission of the European Communities. Communication from the commission to the council and the european parliament - implementing the community strategy to reduce co2 emissions from cars: - fourth annual report on the effectiveness of the strategy (reporting year 2002). Web resource: http://eur-lex.europa.eu/LexUriServ/LexUriServ.do?uri=COM:2004:0078:F IN:EN:PDF, 2004.

[OZ08]   Open-ZB. Open-source toolset for ieee 802.15.4 and zigbee. Web page: http://open-zb.net, 2008.

[PB94]   C. Perkins and P. Bhagwat. Highly dynamic destination-sequenced distance-vector routing (dsdv) for mobile computers. In *Proc. ACM SIGCOMM'94 Conference on Communications Architectures, Protocols and Applications*, pages 234–244, 1994.

[PBRD03]   C. Perkins, E. Belding-Royer, and S. Das. Ad hoc on-demand distance vector (aodv) routing. IETF RFC 3561, July 2003.

[PMGB02]   W.B. Powell, A. Marar, J. Gelfand, and S. Bowers. Implementing real-time optimization models: A case application from the motor carrier industry. *Operations Research*, 50(4):571–581, 2002.

[PMM07]   B. Pasztor, M. Musolesi, and C. Mascolo. Opportunistic mobile sensor data collection with scar. In *Proc. IEEE International Conference on Mobile Ad-hoc and Sensor Systems (MASS) 2007*, pages 1–12, October 2007.

[Psa88]   H.N. Psaraftis. Dynamic vehicle routing problems. In B.L. Golden and A.A. Assad, editors, *Vehicle Routing: Methods and Studies*, pages 223–248. North-Holland, Amsterdam, 1988.

[Rea06]   S. Rea. *Dynamic route management strategies for mobile ad-hoc networks*. PhD thesis, Centre for Adaptive Wireless Systems, Cork Institute of Technology, 2006.

[RLH06]   Y. Rekhter, T. Li, and S. Hares. A border gateway protocol 4 (bgp-4). IETF RFC 4271, January 2006.

[RMSM01]   E.M. Royer, P.M. Melliar-Smith, and L.E. Moser. An analysis of the optimum node density for ad hoc mobile networks. In *IEEE International Conference on Communications (ICC) 2001*, volume 3, pages 857–861, 2001.

[RMSR09]   H. Rekersbrink, T. Makuschwitz, and B. Scholz-Reiter. A distributed routing concept for vehicle routing problems. *Logistics Research*, 1(1):45–52, 2009.

[SAW+04]   B.J. Stocks, M.E. Alexander, B.M. Wotton, C.N. Stefner, M.D. Flannigan, S.W. Taylor, N. Lavoie, J.A. Mason, G.R. Hartley, M.E. Maffey, G.N. Dalrymple, T.W. Blake, M.G. Cruz, and R.A. Lanoville. Crown fire behaviour in a northern jack pine - black spruce forest. *Canadian Journal of Forest Research*, 34(8):1548–1560, 2004.

[Sch04]   J. Schönberger. *Operational Freight Carrier Planning - Investigations on Basic Concepts, Optimization Models and Advanced Memetic Algorithms*. PhD thesis, Chair for Logistics, University of Bremen, 2004.

[Sch05]   A. Schrijver. On the history of combinatorial optimization (till 1960). In K. Aardal, G.L. Nemhauser, and R. Weismantel, editors, *Handbook of Discrete Optimization*, pages 1–68. Elsevier, Amsterdam, 2005.

[SF06]   R. Subramanian and F. Fekri. Sleep scheduling and lifetime maximization in sensor networks: fundamental limits and optimal solutions. In *Proc. 5th international conference on Information processing in sensor networks*, pages 218–225, 2006.

[SLPF03]   T. Strang, C. Linnhoff-Popien, and K. Frank. Cool: A context ontology language to enable contextual interoperability. In J.-B. Stefani, I. Dameure, and D. Hagimont, editors, *LNCS 2893: Proc. 4th IFIP WG 6.1 International Conference on Distributed Applications and Interoperable Systems (DAIS2003)*, volume 2893 of *Lecture Notes in Computer Science (LNCS)*, pages 236–247, November 2003.

[Sol87]   M.M. Solomon. Algorithms for the vehicle routing and scheduling problems with time window constraints. *Operations Research*, 35(2):254–265, 1987.

[SRFR+05]   B. Scholz-Reiter, M. Freitag, H. Rekersbrink, B.-L. Wenning, C. Gorldt, and W. Echelmeyer. Auf dem weg zur selbststeuerung in der logistik - grundlagenforschung und praxisprojekte. In G. Wäscher, K. Inderfurth, G. Neumann, M. Schenk, and D. Ziems, editors, *Intelligente Logistikprozesse - Konzepte, Lösungen, Erfahrungen.Begleitband zur 11. Magdeburger Logistiktagung*, pages 166–180, 2005.

[SRRF06]   B. Scholz-Reiter, H. Rekersbrink, and M. Freitag. Internet routing protocols as an autonomous control approach for transport networks. In R. Teti, editor, *Proc. 5th CIRP international seminar on intelligent computation in manufacturing engineering*, pages 341–345, 2006.

[SRRWM08] B. Scholz-Reiter, H. Rekersbrink, B.-L. Wenning, and T. Makuschewitz. A survey of autonomous control algorithms by means of adapted vehicle routing problems. In *Proc. 9th Biennal ASME Conference on EngineeringSystems Design and Analysis (ESDA 08)*, pages CD–ROM, 6 pages, July 2008.

[SRWF04] B. Scholz-Reiter, K. Windt, and M. Freitag. Autonomous logistic processes: New demands and first approaches. In L. Monostori, editor, *Proc. 37th CIRP international Seminar on Manufacturing Systems*, pages 357–362, 2004.

[ST66] M.D. Springer and W.E. Thompson. The distribution of products of independent random variables. *SIAM Journal on Applied Mathematics*, 14(3):511–526, May 1966.

[SW65] S.S. Shapiro and M.B. Wilk. An analysis of variance test for normality (complete samples). *Biometrika*, 52(3 and 4):591–611, 1965.

[Tex07] Texas Instruments. *CC2420 2.4 GHz IEEE 802.15.4/ZigBee-ready RF transceiver (Rev. B)*, March 2007.

[Tho06] I.J. Thomas. Design, analysis and simulation of a distributed multiple criteria network routing method. Master's thesis, Department of Electrical Engineering and Computer Science, Case Western Reserve University, Cleveland, Ohio, USA, 2006.

[Tin] Tinyaodv implementation. TinyOS source code repository: http://tinyos.cvs. sourceforge.net/viewvc/tinyos/tinyos-1.x/contrib/hsn/.

[Tin08] Tinyos community forum. Web page: http://www.tinyos.net, 2008.

[WBP05] K. Windt, F. Böse, and T. Philipp. Criteria and application of autonomous cooperating logistic processes. In J.X. Gao, D.I. Baxter, and P.J. Sackett, editors, *Proc. 3rd International Conference on Manufacturing Research . Advances in Manufacturing Technology and Management*, 2005.

[WGP05] B.-L. Wenning, C. Görg, and K. Peters. Ereignisdiskrete modellierung von selbststeuerung in transportnetzen. *Industrie Management*, 21(5):53–56, 2005.

[WLTG⁺08] B.-L. Wenning, A. Lukosius, A. Timm-Giel, C. Görg, and S. Tomic. Opportunistic distance-aware routing in multi-sink mobile wireless sensor networks. In *Proc. ICT-MobileSummit 2008*, pages CD–ROM, 8 pages, June 2008.

[WPTG06] B.-L. Wenning, D. Pesch, and A. Timm-Giel. A distributed routing approach for vehicle routing in logistic networks. In *Proc. 64th IEEE Vehicular Technology Conference*, pages CD–ROM, 5 pages, September 2006.

[WPTGG08] B.-L. Wenning, D. Pesch, A. Timm-Giel, and C. Görg. Environmental monitoring aware routing in wireless sensor networks. In *Proc. 10th IFIP Conference on Mobile and Wireless Communications Networks (MWCN)*, pages 5–16, September 2008.

[WPTGG09] B.-L. Wenning, D. Pesch, A. Timm-Giel, and C. Görg. Environmental monitoring aware routing: Making environmental sensor networks more robust. *Telecommunication Systems*, 43(1):3–11, 2009.

[WRTG⁺07] B.-L. Wenning, H. Rekersbrink, A. Timm-Giel, C. Görg, and B. Scholz-Reiter. Autonomous control by means of distributed routing. In M. Hülsmann and K. Windt, editors, *Understanding Autonomous Cooperation and Control in Logistics - The Impact on Management, Information and Communication and Material Flow*, pages 325–335. Springer, 2007.

[WRTGG09] B.-L. Wenning, H. Rekersbrink, A. Timm-Giel, and C. Görg. Weighted multiplicative decision function for distributed routing in transport logistics. In *Proc. 2nd international conference on dynamics in logistics (LDIC 2009)*, page to appear, 2009.

[WTGG09] B.-L. Wenning, A. Timm-Giel, and C. Görg. A generic framework for context-aware routing and its implementation in wireless sensor networks. In *Mobilkommunikation - Technologien und Anwendungen, Vorträge der 14. ITG Fachtagung*, pages 53–58, May 2009.

[YF04] O. Younis and S. Fahmi. Heed: a hybrid, energy-efficient, distributed clustering approach for ad hoc sensor networks. *IEEE Transactions on Mobile Computing*, 3(4):366–379, 2004.

Advanced Studies Mobile Research Center Bremen

Herausgeber: Prof. Dr. Otthein Herzog, Prof. Dr. Carmelita Görg, Prof. Dr.-Ing. Bernd Scholz-Reiter

Hans-Florian Geerdes
UMTS Radio Network Planning: Mastering Cell Coupling for Capacity Optimization
2008. x, 186 pp. with 54 Fig. and 31 Tab. Softc. EUR 45,90
ISBN 978-3-8348-0697-0

Eugen Lamers
Contributions to Simulation Speed-Up
Rare Event Simulation and Short-Term Dynamic Simulation for Mobile Network Planning
2008. xxi, 148 pp. with 57 Fig. and 11 Tab, Softc. EUR 45,90
ISBN 978-3-8348-0524-9

Andreas Könsgen
Design and Simulation of Spectrum Management Methods for Wireless Local Area Networks
2010. xxv, 236 pp. with 108 Fig. and 20 Tab. Softc. EUR 49,95
ISBN 978-3-8348-1244-5

Bernd-Ludwig Wenning
Context-Based Routing in Dynamic Networks
2010. xxv, 187 pp. with 60 Fig. and 18 Tab. Softc. EUR 49,95
ISBN 978-3-8348-1295-7

VIEWEG+
TEUBNER

Abraham-Lincoln-Straße 46
65189 Wiesbaden
Fax 0611.7878-400
www.viewegteubner.de

Stand April 2010.
Änderungen vorbehalten.
Erhältlich im Buchhandel oder im Verlag.

CPSIA information can be obtained at www.ICGtesting.com
Printed in the USA
LVOW060211240113

317018LV00008B/215/P